"With *Eating in the Middle*, Andie is squashing the all-
or-nothing dieting attitude one recipe at a time. You
can feel her vibrant and genuine spirit in each word.
In fact, Andie is your best friend on this journey with
you. I've never seen a cookbook celebrate a realistic,
healthful lifestyle (with the occasionally indulgence!)
as well as *Eating in the Middle*. Fabulous!"

—JESSICA MERCHANT, author of *Seriously Delish* and blogger
at HowSweetEats.com

"Anyone who is or wants to be a mindful eater will
treasure *Eating in the Middle*, as moderation has never
been more approachable and satisfying. Those who
loved Andie's memoir, *It Was Me All Along*, will be
thrilled that she's back with another work as honest as
it is delicious."

—KERRY DIAMOND, cofounder of *Cherry Bombe* magazine

"Andie Mitchell makes balance possible for us all in her
new book by reimagining her favorite dishes and foods
for a modern (and moderate) lifestyle."

—CLAUDIA WU, cofounder of *Cherry Bombe* magazine

"As someone who has obsessed over food my whole
life, in both positive and challenging ways, I felt that
reading Andie's words was like hearing the voice
inside of my head. I'm sure I'm not the only one to feel
that way. Once again, just like she did in her moving
memoir, Andie gives us so much. Not only are there
recipes that will make you want to get in the kitchen
immediately, there's that honest and vulnerable
voice that makes us feel less alone in the struggle to
maintain healthy relationships with both food and
ourselves."

—JULIA TURSHEN, cookbook writer

Eating in the Middle

Eating in the Middle

A MOSTLY WHOLESOME COOKBOOK

ANDIE MITCHELL

Author of the *New York Times* bestselling memoir *It Was Me All Along*

PHOTOGRAPHS BY ARAN GOYOAGA

Clarkson Potter/Publishers
New York

ISBN 978-0-7704-3327-7
eBook ISBN 978-0-7704-3328-4

Printed in China

Book and cover design by Danielle Deschenes
Cover photographs by Aran Goyoaga
Prop styling by Jenn Elliot-Blake
Kitchen assistant: Jessie Blount

10 9 8 7 6 5 4 3 2 1

First Edition

Daniel,
You are my solid ground. No matter where we go,
I'll love you everywhere, all the time.

Contents

INTRODUCTION 9

STARTING FRESH 13

LUNCHTIME 45

VEGETABLES & SIDES 77

DINNERTIME 105

FOR SHARING 165

ALL THINGS SWEET 197

ACKNOWLEDGMENTS 236

INDEX 237

INTRODUCTION

* 🌼 *

Ten years ago, I began my weight loss journey—one that lasted for thirteen humbling months and concluded when I'd lost 135 pounds. It was the most transformative experience of my life—and not simply in the ways one might expect. Of course, I had changed my body dramatically, but the work didn't stop there. I also had to tackle the harder task of transforming my relationship with my body and eating.

It's easy to see that I've always loved food. The photos of me from childhood are full of me and brownies, me and pasta, me and cake. In my mother's attic, I have stowed a box—an "Important box," as I articulately wrote on it with permanent marker some years ago. In it are things I've collected that have special meaning to me. These are the only things that I'd want to save if the house were on fire—birthday cards from my brother, a poem from my first love, letters that my dad wrote to me from Arizona before he passed away, old photos, my favorite art projects, and so on. And there are recipes in that box. Lots are handwritten and tattered, creased and folded so many times that they could tear at any moment. Either my mom jotted them down quickly on the backs of envelopes, or my nana did on some faded index card. There are even magazine-clipped recipes from 1978, the year my brother was born, when Mom first learned to cook and, in some cosmic way, started teaching me. I love these recipes like I love certain people in my life. I know them. I talk about them. I can be reminded of them. And when they're gone, I miss them.

But even loving food and recipes as much as I do, I can't say my relationship with eating has always been peaceful, or easy, or even normal. I spent two decades—the first twenty years of my life—eating like mad. I ate for so many reasons, and most of them were completely unrelated to hunger or a lack of fullness. I distracted myself with eating. I comforted myself with it, turned to eating when I was bored, and stuffed myself when I needed to feel anything but the pain of a hard childhood.

The year I turned twenty, I found my five-foot-nine self standing on a scale at the YMCA and staring down at 268 pounds. Terrified isn't a strong enough word for how scared I was. The weight was more real in that moment than it had ever been. The choice to change was clearer, more desperate than it had been before.

That was 2005, the year I turned my life around. And by the middle of 2006, I had lost 135 pounds.

For a long while, I struggled with not knowing how to eat to maintain such a loss. *Is life a constant diet?* I wondered. I missed the foods I'd always loved—the richer, heavier comfort dishes—the ones I'd avoided while losing. Now I just couldn't imagine how I'd ever be able to incorporate such things into the new, healthier life I'd created. It was the constant pressure to maintain the loss that drove me to insanity. Slowly, though, I began to realize that if one goal of changing myself was to feel happier, I was failing to achieve that. To really dig into this emotional side of the struggle, I went to therapy, where I began the amazing and grueling work of unpacking all the things I'd attached to food. Gradually, I began to understand the triggers that caused me to eat without a shred of control—and I started to teach myself to weather my emotions without eating.

As I got the hang of the emotional side of eating, I still felt like something was missing. I realized I needed to address the practical side of those nagging cravings for the foods I'd always loved but that I'd banned myself from eating while I was losing weight. I didn't want to live the rest of my life devoid of desserts. I didn't want to go to family parties and feel nervous about how many calories were in the lasagna. Maybe it was time to stop dreaming about moderation and start living it. And with that, I went back to the kitchen.

I started cooking. I experimented with healthier versions of classic recipes that my mom always made, which meant a whole lot of lightening—sometimes successfully and sometimes so, so poorly. I ended up with more than a few "lighter" carrot cakes that were as dense and heavy as tires. In the process, I accidentally set things on fire, burned my hands when I forgot pot holders, and blistered my arms with steam. I used baking soda in place of baking powder 634 times. It was crazy and, somehow, magical. But I learned to cook—and not just to butter and salt and sugar everything until it tastes good because of the deliciousness of butter and salt and sugar—but to really *cook*. To season, to spice. And I learned to nourish myself. What I found in the end was that working to make the meal—going on the journey from shopping to chopping to cooking to plating—made me not want to overeat nearly as much. I wanted to savor what I'd made. I wanted to share it. Finally, I realized I wasn't just having fun making meals; I was rebooting my relationship with food. I was reconciling my past with my future.

The more I've learned about myself through cooking, the more balance I've found. And while balance looks and feels different for each of us, for me it's about living a full, vibrant life where no food is off the table. I love kale, green juices, and hemp seeds, and I believe in eating a giant salad once a day, but I don't want to be deprived of the rest of the food in the world. I can't even bear to imagine a life where doughnuts are not an option. The style of eating that I practice keeps me sane and feeling good—but better than that, it keeps me happy. There's no compulsive cycle of dieting and overdoing it. Not anymore, anyway. Now, there's a middle ground, where most of the time I'm making my own meals with an abundance of wholesome, good-for-me ingredients, and other times I'm springing for the loaded chorizo nachos with my friends because it's Friday and we're nothing if not celebratory.

Eating in the Middle is structured the way I eat and live my life. So, the vast majority of the recipes in this book are healthy, wholesome, and made from real-food ingredients, with a focus on big, boisterous flavors. You'd swear most of them are richer than they are, like Lemon-Herb Fish with Crispy Oven Fries (page 110), Beef Puttanesca with Garlic Bread (page 133) , and Spaghetti with Brussels Sprouts & Pancetta Cream (page 145). And then, there are two chapters—For Sharing (page 164) and All Things Sweet (page 196)—with recipes that are richer and more decadent. For Sharing is full of the kinds of things you'd make on the weekends, when you have friends or family over for dinner—Lemon Cream Risotto (page 195), Cuban Pulled-Pork Sandwiches with Caramelized Onion & Thyme Mayo (page 181), Meatloaf Burgers with Bacon, Pepper Jack & Frizzled Onions (page 169). They're meals for gathering, with hearty, stick-to-your-ribs appeal. And the desserts in All Things Sweet are also as rich as can be. Skillet Apple Crisp with Whiskey Caramel Sauce (page 215) and Dulce de Leche Cream-Filled Doughnuts with Chocolate Glaze (page 225)—they're celebrations in and of themselves. I serve these on special occasions, or any time there's a need for lots of sharing.

This book, and the way it breaks down into mostly wholesome with a sprinkling of decadence, is exactly how I live my life. It's balance. It's the testament of a life well-lived, with plenty of real, whole foods and some life-changing Chocolate Hazelnut Bread Pudding (page 233) thrown in there, too.

For those of us who struggle or have struggled with eating or weight, the ultimate work is finding a way to mend our relationship with food. *Eating in the Middle* can't heal your relationship, but it can read as a love story of balance. If I've learned one thing in these thirty years, it's that you can be healthy, happy, and feel good while eating food that you crave. I hope this book nudges you into the kitchen, that the pages become stained with oils and touched by sticky fingers, that you write in the margins as you make the recipes your own. But more than anything, I hope that cooking teaches you something about your own sense of balance, and that you feel just fine about loving food as much as you do.

Starting Fresh

BAKED BANANA BREAD DOUGHNUTS, *page 16*

BAKED BANANA BREAD
DOUGHNUTS 16

GREEK YOGURT PANCAKES 19

TURKEY BREAKFAST PATTIES 22

CHOCOLATE RASPBERRY
BREAKFAST PUDDING 25

TOMORROATS WITH BLOOD
ORANGE MINT SALSA 26

BREAKFAST EGG SALAD 31

ALL THE GREENS FRITTATA 33

PEANUT BUTTER
GRANOLA PARFAITS 34

MORNING GLORY MUFFINS 37

CREAMY SPINACH,
SUN-DRIED TOMATO &
ARTICHOKE OMELET 38

TWICE-BAKED
BREAKFAST POTATOES 40

SWEET POTATO HASH 43

BAKED BANANA BREAD DOUGHNUTS

I am wild about doughnuts. I've hunted them down at the most buzzed-about shops in various states, waited in long lines at road-side carts, and have even requested a tower of doughnuts in lieu of cake for my birthday (you only turn thirty once!). My favorites are the loud, over-the-top cream-filled ones, and because of that, I try to save them for a special dessert. So for breakfast, I came up with this recipe for a lighter baked version. These cake doughnuts combine all the sweet, tender qualities of a soft banana bread with warm, cinnamon-spice flavor—and each is just over one hundred calories, unglazed. On weekends, though, I like to frost them with a light maple-cinnamon cream cheese glaze, just to make things special.

---

1 Preheat the oven to 350°F. Spray a standard nonstick doughnut pan with nonstick cooking spray.

2 In a medium bowl, whisk together the flour, baking powder, cinnamon, nutmeg, allspice, cloves, and salt.

3 In a large bowl, whisk together the milk, oil, egg, vanilla, sugar, and mashed bananas. Slowly add the flour mixture to the banana mixture and stir until just combined. Carefully spoon the batter into the doughnut pan, filling each mold nearly to the top.

4 Bake until the doughnuts spring back when gently pressed, 12 to 15 minutes. Turn the doughnuts out onto a wire rack to cool completely.

5 Drizzle approximately 1 tablespoon of the glaze over each cooled doughnut and let set for 10 minutes before serving. These doughnuts will keep in an airtight container at room temperature for up to 5 days.

Makes 12; serves 12

PER SERVING	
Calories	170
Protein	3 g
Carbohydrates	29 g
Fiber	3 g
Sugar	15 g
Total Fat	6 g
Saturated Fat	1 g
Sodium	156 mg

1¾ cups whole-wheat flour

1½ teaspoons baking powder

1½ teaspoons ground cinnamon

¼ teaspoon ground nutmeg

¼ teaspoon allspice

⅛ teaspoon ground cloves

½ teaspoon salt

½ cup unsweetened almond milk

¼ cup vegetable oil

1 large egg, lightly beaten

1 teaspoon pure vanilla extract

½ cup packed light brown sugar

3 medium very ripe bananas, mashed (about 1¼ cups)

Maple-Cinnamon Cream Cheese Glaze (recipe follows)

PER TABLESPOON	
Calories	40
Protein	1 g
Carbohydrates	4 g
Fiber	0 g
Sugar	4 g
Total Fat	3 g
Saturated Fat	2 g
Sodium	43 mg

Maple-Cinnamon Cream Cheese Glaze

Makes a scant ½ cup

3 ounces ⅓ less fat cream cheese, at room temperature

2 tablespoons pure maple syrup

Splash of pure vanilla extract

Pinch of ground cinnamon

———————

In a small bowl, whisk together the cream cheese, syrup, vanilla, and cinnamon until smooth.

GREEK YOGURT PANCAKES

Makes 12 4-inch pancakes; serves 6

PER SERVING	
Calories	298
Protein	8 g
Carbohydrates	59 g
Fiber	3 g
Sugar	27 g
Total Fat	4 g
Saturated Fat	1 g
Sodium	600 mg

I grew up eating pancakes made from a boxed mix, and even so, they were such a treat. These days, I make my own from scratch, which isn't as labor intensive as it sounds, and the resulting pancakes are so soft and pillowy that you'll never go back to boxed. And these pancakes are much healthier, too, with Greek yogurt to keep them tender and a blend of whole-wheat and all-purpose flours to get in some extra fiber.

I have a new syrup technique: dipping! I make a pool of syrup next to my pancakes and dip each bite. That way, the pancakes don't absorb excess syrup, which you can't taste anyway, and I don't end up pouring on more and more. Now I get the flavor without the extra calories and sugar.

1 cup whole-wheat flour

1 cup all-purpose flour

4 teaspoons baking powder

1 tablespoon sugar

½ teaspoon salt

1½ cups unsweetened almond milk

2 large eggs

2 teaspoons pure vanilla extract

½ cup plain 2% Greek yogurt

¾ cup pure maple syrup, for serving

1 In a large bowl, whisk together the flours, baking powder, sugar, and salt.

2 In a small bowl, whisk together the milk, eggs, and vanilla. Pour the liquid mixture into the flour mixture and stir just until combined. Add the yogurt and stir.

3 Heat a 12-inch nonstick skillet or griddle over medium heat and spray it well with nonstick cooking spray. Working in batches, spoon a quarter cup of the batter onto the pan for each pancake and cook just until bubbles form around the edges of each pancake, about 3 minutes. Flip and cook for 90 seconds more. Transfer the pancakes to a warm plate. Repeat with the remaining batter.

4 Divide the pancakes among 6 plates and serve each stack with a small bowl filled with 2 tablespoons of maple syrup.

TURKEY BREAKFAST PATTIES

All through college, I had a love affair with sausage-egg-and-cheese bagel sandwiches. I just couldn't stop myself from getting them at all hours—especially since my favorite drive-through coffee shop served them twenty-four hours a day. Naturally, one part of beginning to lose weight was breaking this habit and finding new ways to enjoy this favorite more moderately—especially without adding a doughnut on the side. These spiced turkey patties scratch the itch for traditional pork sausage for a fraction of the calories. To prevent the patties from drying out (since the turkey is so lean), I added grated zucchini. Serve these alongside a wedge of All the Greens Frittata (page 33).

Makes 8 patties; serves 4

PER SERVING

Calories	172
Protein	24 g
Carbohydrates	5 g
Fiber	1 g
Total Fat	6 g
Saturated Fat	1 g
Sodium	502 mg

1 pound ground turkey breast

1 tablespoon pure maple syrup

2 scallions, white and light-green parts, finely chopped

½ cup grated zucchini

2 garlic cloves, minced

½ teaspoon ground sage

¾ teaspoon fennel seeds

½ teaspoon dried thyme

Pinch of allspice

¾ teaspoon salt

¼ teaspoon freshly ground black pepper

4 teaspoons extra-virgin olive oil

1 In a large bowl, combine the turkey, maple syrup, scallions, zucchini, garlic, sage, fennel, thyme, allspice, salt, and pepper. Using your hands, shape the mixture into 8 patties.

2 In a 12-inch nonstick skillet, heat 2 teaspoons of the oil over medium-high heat. Add 4 of the patties and cook until golden brown and crisp, 3 to 4 minutes. Flip and cook the other side for 3 to 4 more minutes. Transfer the patties to a warm plate.

3 Repeat with the remaining 4 patties. Divide the patties among 4 plates and serve.

CHOCOLATE RASPBERRY
BREAKFAST PUDDING

I went through a phase in which I ate oatmeal every day for, oh, I don't know, a year straight? A year and a half? I'm just one of those people who can eat the same thing day after day (after day after day . . .) and like it quite a bit. My dad was like this. My brother is, too. But then, all of a sudden, I'll find myself—on the seven thousandth day—biting into the same ol' oatmeal, and it's as if a switch flips. "What am I *eating*?!" And just like that, I'm done with the oats.

I began a chia seed phase when my oat phase ended, and I'm really loving it. This pudding is lightly sweetened with maple syrup and is slightly creamy. Chia seeds double in size when you soak them, making them extremely hydrating and filling.

Serves 4

PER SERVING	
Calories	256
Protein	11 g
Carbohydrates	35 g
Fiber	13 g
Sugar	20 g
Total Fat	11 g
Saturated Fat	3 g
Sodium	116 mg

1½ cups unsweetened vanilla almond milk

1½ cups plain 2% Greek yogurt

3 tablespoons unsweetened cocoa powder

¼ cup pure maple syrup

⅓ cup chia seeds

2 cups fresh raspberries, for serving

2 tablespoons unsweetened coconut flakes, for serving

1 In a medium bowl, whisk together the almond milk, yogurt, cocoa powder, maple syrup, and chia seeds. Let stand for 30 minutes. Stir to redistribute the chia seeds. Cover the bowl and refrigerate overnight.

2 In the morning, divide the pudding among 4 small bowls and top with the fresh raspberries and coconut flakes.

TOMORROATS WITH BLOOD ORANGE MINT SALSA

The one part I hate about making a pot of oatmeal on the stovetop every morning is . . . making a pot of oatmeal on the stovetop every morning. I've tried microwaving the oats, but the unfortunate truth is that microwaved oatmeal is never the same; the oats are never as thoroughly puffed, never quite as creamy.

Enter "tomorroats." This type of oatmeal has all the volume, all the creaminess, and none of the fuss. You can even make it a few days in advance, store it refrigerated in sealed containers, and then enjoy quick-and-easy breakfasts on the go. Topped with a minted orange salsa, it's one of my favorite breakfasts!

Serves 4

PER SERVING	
Calories	368
Protein	14 g
Carbohydrates	64 g
Fiber	7 g
Sugar	32 g
Total Fat	7 g
Saturated Fat	2 g
Sodium	154 mg

2 cups old-fashioned rolled oats

2 cups unsweetened almond milk (or dairy milk)

2 cups plain 2% Greek yogurt (or any plain yogurt you like)

¼ cup pure maple syrup

1 teaspoon pure vanilla extract

Blood Orange Mint Salsa (recipe follows)

1   In a large bowl, combine the oats, milk, yogurt, syrup, and vanilla, and mix well. Divide the mixture among 4 small containers, cover, and refrigerate for at least 6 hours and up to 24 hours.

2   In the morning, top each serving with ½ cup of the salsa and serve.

Blood Orange Mint Salsa

Makes just over 2 cups; serves 4

PER SERVING	
Calories	69
Protein	1 g
Carbohydrates	16 g
Fiber	2 g
Sugar	13 g
Total Fat	0 g
Saturated Fat	0 g
Sodium	1 mg

3 blood oranges, peeled and cut into ½-inch pieces

1 tablespoon finely chopped fresh mint leaves

1 tablespoon honey

Pinch of salt

———————

In a medium bowl, combine the orange pieces, mint, honey, and salt. Cover the bowl and refrigerate for at least 30 minutes and up to 3 days.

CHOOSING BREAKFAST

* 🌻 *

In college, my favorite meal, and the only one my friends and I met for religiously, was brunch. We'd all still be exhausted, never having quite adapted to early morning classes, and each of us would stand outside the dining hall building, waiting until the other three got there to go in together. We'd grab trays, disband to fill plates as if we were preparing for the last day on earth, and then pile into one big booth. Once we were at that table, the dining hall might as well have been empty. We had locked ourselves inside our own conversation and thrown away the key, laughing. No one minded when one of us stole a hash brown from someone else's plate or when I swiped the last strip of bacon.

Walking into my dining hall before noon meant I had free rein over a waffle maker, stacks of hot French toast, pancakes, crispy hash browns, bacon, sausage, a made-to-order omelet station, bagels, fruit, yogurt, and cereal. That's the short list. My favorite breakfast was a toasted bagel sandwich layered with scrambled eggs, a sausage patty, and two slices of melted American cheese. I'd fill the plate surrounding the sandwich with as many hash browns as would fit. On another plate, I'd get a slice of French toast and float it in maple syrup.

At the end of my sophomore year, I could feel my pants—the ones I swore I'd never outgrow—digging into my sides. Their snugness was one of so many signs that it might be time to change my all-you-can-eat ways. The next time I stepped inside the dining hall for brunch, I immediately wished it weren't one enormous buffet. I wanted to try to be healthy this time, but I stood there, daunted by the soft-serve machine alone. Sweet, savory, hot, cold . . . *where do I even start?* I walked through the room with my empty tray as if I'd never been there before, surveying each item. *Why is this so hard?* I wondered. I began mentally listing all the things I would have gotten had this not been the first day I'd ever practiced self-restraint, and when I realized what a hodgepodge it was, a funny question came: *Had I ever really made a choice, or had I just gotten one of everything? And if I had gotten one of everything, could I possibly have wanted all of it?* Probably not.

It was time I started making choices. And good ones.

From then on, when I wanted something on the sweeter side, I filled a bowl with plain yogurt, a sliced banana, fresh berries, and then sprinkled granola on top. On savory days, I waited in line for a two-egg omelet with all the veggies. Sometimes I re-created my favorite breakfast sandwich, with toasted whole-grain

bread, bacon instead of sausage, and one slice of cheese rather than two. The only brunch thing I quit cold turkey was the soft-serve machine. I know . . . it should never have been a thing to begin with. If I craved something richer, I had a few hash browns, or even a half a bagel. Slowly I was realizing that maybe the key to having it all was just not having it all at once, in the form of a sandwich, with hash browns.

When I'd eaten this way long enough, I started to notice that making one small good decision in the morning made me want to make another, and another . . . all day long. Instead of heading back to my dorm room to nap after we'd eat—as I'd so often done between classes, I'd take a walk. At dinner, I'd walk past the french fries to the salad bar with greater ease. I felt better, stronger, and more confident.

Growing up, I'd eaten cereal before school or grabbed a pack of Pop-Tarts in a rush. Breakfast was an afterthought. But now that I was making better choices and feeling the positive effects of them, breakfast became a priority. It was the way I set the tone for my whole day. And even now, years later, I wake up and crave all the positive momentum of a healthy breakfast. I just love knowing that one good decision makes another, and that it all starts right there, in my kitchen.

BREAKFAST EGG SALAD

Why aren't more of us eating egg salad in the morning? I only waited twenty-nine years to ask myself this question and, well, here we are. When we know better, we do better, right? I wanted to make this egg salad taste as rich as the traditional version we all grew up with, so I used half real full-fat mayo, for flavor and creaminess, and half low-fat Greek yogurt, to save calories. If you don't love the taste of Greek yogurt, don't worry, there's almost no detectable tanginess—just an added touch of brightness. And I couldn't resist mixing in salty, smoky crumbled bacon. It is breakfast, after all.

Makes about 2 cups; serves 4

PER SERVING	
Calories	278
Protein	16 g
Carbohydrates	14 g
Fiber	2 g
Sugar	3 g
Total Fat	17 g
Saturated Fat	4 g
Sodium	523 mg

1 Put the eggs in a medium saucepan, cover with 1 inch of water, and bring to a boil over high heat. Remove the pan from the heat, cover, and let stand for 12 minutes. Immediately transfer the eggs to an ice bath for 5 minutes. Peel and chop the eggs.

2 In a medium bowl, combine the eggs, mayonnaise, yogurt, mustard, bacon, red onion, chives, salt, and pepper. Serve on toast. The egg salad will keep in an airtight container in the refrigerator for 1 day.

6 large eggs

2 tablespoons full-fat mayonnaise

2 tablespoons plain 2% Greek yogurt

2 teaspoons Dijon mustard

4 slices cooked bacon, crumbled

3 tablespoons finely chopped red onion

1 tablespoon finely chopped fresh chives

¼ teaspoon salt

¼ teaspoon freshly ground black pepper

4 pieces 100% whole-grain bread, toasted

ALL THE GREENS FRITTATA

I dragged my feet on joining the frittata bandwagon. Something about the lack of a crust just bummed me out. But over time I realized that when I made a flavorful enough frittata, I wasn't missing anything at all—I was just as satisfied *and* I'd saved calories. This frittata is garlicky and fragrant with basil, with just the right amount of punch from the creamy goat cheese.

1   Preheat the oven to 350°F.

2   In a medium bowl, beat the eggs. Set aside.

3   In a 10-inch ovenproof nonstick skillet, heat the oil over medium-high heat. Add the shallots, asparagus, leeks, salt, and pepper, and cook until beginning to brown, about 5 minutes.

4   Add the spinach and cook, stirring frequently, until wilted, 1 to 2 minutes. Lower the heat to medium, add the garlic, and cook, stirring constantly, until fragrant, 30 seconds.

5   Add the eggs and stir. Cook, without stirring, until just set on the bottom, 30 to 45 seconds. Using a plastic spatula, lift the frittata edge nearest to you and tilt the skillet gently so that the eggs run underneath the cooked bottom. Swirl the pan to evenly distribute the egg in the skillet and continue to cook for 1 minute. Lift the pan once more to repeat the process until the egg on top is no longer runny. Scatter the goat cheese on top.

6   Bake until the top is set and the cheese begins to melt, 5 to 7 minutes. Sprinkle the basil over the top.

7   Run a spatula around the sides of the frittata and transfer it to a large serving plate. Cut into four pieces and serve warm, at room temperature, or even chilled.

Serves 4

PER SERVING	
Calories	253
Protein	16 g
Carbohydrates	12 g
Fiber	2 g
Sugar	4 g
Total Fat	16 g
Saturated Fat	6 g
Sodium	472 mg

6 large eggs

1 tablespoon extra-virgin olive oil

1 medium shallot, finely chopped (about ¼ cup)

½ pound asparagus, trimmed and cut into 1-inch pieces (about 1 cup)

2 large leeks, white and light-green parts only, halved lengthwise and cut into ½-inch-thick pieces (about 2 cups)

½ teaspoon salt

¼ teaspoon freshly ground black pepper

2½ ounces baby spinach leaves (2 packed cups)

2 garlic cloves, minced

2 ounces goat cheese, crumbled (about ½ cup)

2 tablespoons finely chopped fresh basil leaves

PEANUT BUTTER GRANOLA PARFAITS

This one is for the non-morning people, the folks with rushed a.m. routines, and those who flat-out wake up because breakfast exists. How is that, you ask? Because it's quick; it's ready when you are; it can be prepared ahead of time, grabbed on the go—and it hits every craving: sweet, a little salty, creamy, crunchy. If you're a peanut butter lover, you've got to try this. Your morning is about to get a whole lot more lovable.

_____

1 For the granola, preheat the oven to 300°F. Line a large rimmed baking sheet with parchment paper.

2 In a medium bowl, combine the oats and peanuts.

3 In a small microwave-safe bowl, combine the peanut butter and honey. Microwave on high until melted, about 30 seconds. Stir in the cinnamon and salt. Stir the mixture into the oats and peanuts. Spread the oats onto the prepared baking sheet.

4 Bake, stirring every few minutes to prevent burning, until golden, about 10 minutes. Transfer the baking sheet to a wire rack and let the granola cool, stirring occasionally. When cool, transfer the granola to an airtight container and store at room temperature for up to 3 weeks.

5 For the parfaits, in each of 4 small Mason jars or small bowls, layer ½ cup of the yogurt, an eighth of the sliced bananas, 2 tablespoons granola, then another ½ cup of the yogurt, another eighth of the sliced bananas, and another 2 tablespoons granola. Serve immediately or cover and refrigerate for up to 3 days.

Makes 1 cup; serves 4

PER SERVING	
Calories	396
Protein	22 g
Carbohydrates	49 g
Fiber	4 g
Sugar	33 g
Total Fat	15 g
Saturated Fat	5 g
Sodium	305 mg

Granola
¾ cup old-fashioned rolled oats
¼ cup chopped roasted unsalted peanuts
2 tablespoons creamy natural peanut butter
2 tablespoons honey
½ teaspoon ground cinnamon
¼ teaspoon salt

Parfaits
4 cups plain 2% Greek yogurt or your favorite low-fat plain yogurt
2 large bananas, sliced

MORNING GLORY MUFFINS

I think there was a time for all of us when we ate muffins with abandon. They were softball size, left oil rings on their paper liners, and kept us full for no amount of time whatsoever. We might have transitioned to bran muffins or even reduced-fat blueberry ones, thinking we were being healthy. And then, somewhere along the way, we were informed that those muffins . . . were 400 calories each. We were shocked and sad. And then we sighed, missing them already.

Let's not give them up. Let's just find ones that are better for us *most* of the time. These muffins are made entirely with whole-wheat flour and are loaded with some good-for-you mix-ins, such as carrots, pineapple, raisins, and coconut.

_____

1 Preheat the oven to 350°F. Line 18 standard muffin tin cups with paper liners.

2 In a large bowl, whisk together the flour, sugar, baking soda, baking powder, cinnamon, and salt.

3 In the bowl of a stand mixer fitted with the whisk attachment, beat the oil, eggs, and pineapple. Add the flour mixture and beat until just combined. Using a spatula, stir in the carrots, raisins, and coconut. Scoop the batter into the prepared muffin cups, filling each three-quarters full.

4 Bake until a toothpick inserted into the center of a muffin comes out clean, about 20 minutes. Transfer the muffins to a wire rack and let cool. Serve warm or at room temperature. The muffins will keep in an airtight container at room temperature for up to 4 days.

Makes 18; serves 18

PER SERVING	
Calories	187
Protein	4 g
Carbohydrates	26 g
Fiber	3 g
Sugar	14 g
Total Fat	9 g
Saturated Fat	3 g
Sodium	230 mg

2¼ cups whole-wheat flour

⅔ cup sugar

1½ teaspoons baking soda

½ teaspoon baking powder

1 teaspoon ground cinnamon

¾ teaspoon salt

½ cup vegetable oil

3 large eggs

1 8-ounce can crushed pineapple

3 large carrots, shredded (about 1½ cups)

½ cup raisins

½ cup unsweetened shredded coconut

CREAMY SPINACH, SUN-DRIED TOMATO & ARTICHOKE OMELET

The hot spinach-and-artichoke dip commonly found at restaurants is downright delicious, but it's also one of those appetizers I can easily lose myself in. The heady garlic-Parmesan flavor, the creaminess, the crunchy toasted bread . . . everything about it just works for me. The one trouble, of course, is that it's an entire day's worth of calories in one cute little bowl. This omelet is a healthier tribute to that creamy app. It packs in all the signature ingredients, with a sweet kick from sun-dried tomatoes, and it even takes on that rich, creamy texture thanks to dollops of cream cheese that melt inside the fold. For a more complete meal, try serving the omelet with a Turkey Breakfast Patty (page 22) on the side!

Serves 2

PER SERVING	
Calories	301
Protein	20 g
Carbohydrates	10 g
Fiber	3 g
Sugar	2 g
Total Fat	21 g
Saturated Fat	8 g
Sodium	599 mg

8 large egg whites

Pinch of freshly ground black pepper

2 teaspoons extra-virgin olive oil

2½ ounces baby spinach leaves (2 packed cups)

4 canned artichoke hearts, chopped

2 sun-dried tomatoes packed in olive oil, drained, pressed dry with a paper towel, and finely chopped (about ¼ cup)

2 ounces ⅓ less fat cream cheese, at room temperature, cut into small chunks

4 teaspoons grated Parmesan cheese

1 In a small bowl, beat 4 egg whites with a pinch of pepper.

2 In a small nonstick skillet, heat 1 teaspoon of the oil over medium-high heat. Add 1 cup of the spinach and cook, stirring frequently, until wilted, about 1 minute.

3 Add half the artichoke hearts, half the sun-dried tomatoes, and the egg whites. Stir to combine them with the spinach and cook, without stirring, until the eggs are opaque and beginning to set, 1 to 2 minutes.

4 Drop half of the cream cheese chunks along one side of the omelet. Turn off the heat and fold the side of the omelet that doesn't have the cream cheese over onto the other half. Transfer to a warm serving plate and sprinkle the top with 2 teaspoons of the Parmesan cheese.

5 Beat the remaining 4 egg whites in the bowl, season with another pinch of pepper, and repeat the cooking process with the remaining ingredients. Serve immediately.

TWICE-BAKED BREAKFAST POTATOES

For a little while after college, I worked as a waitress at a steakhouse. During the twenty minutes or so of my shift when I didn't feel I was failing miserably at the whole job, I would lust after the twice-baked potatoes that people ordered alongside their steaks. One day, it dawned on me that all the things involved in twice-baked potatoes are also found together on my breakfast plate—only with the addition of scrambled eggs. And, voilà! I made breakfast out of a steakhouse special! This recipe has all the makings of a good morning—scrambled eggs, bacon, Cheddar cheese, and potato—in one little package.

_____

1 Preheat the oven to 400°F.

2 Prick each potato several times with a fork, place on a large rimmed baking sheet, and bake until tender, about 1 hour.

3 In a 12-inch nonstick skillet set over medium-high heat, cook the bacon until crisp, 5 to 7 minutes. Transfer to a paper towel–lined plate to drain. Wipe out the skillet.

4 In a small bowl, beat the eggs with a pinch each of salt and pepper.

5 In the same skillet, melt the butter over medium heat. Add the eggs and cook, stirring frequently with a rubber spatula, until large curds form and the eggs are no longer runny, 2 to 3 minutes. Transfer to a small bowl.

6 When the potatoes are cool enough to handle, cut each potato in half lengthwise and scoop out the flesh into a small bowl, leaving a ¼-inch border. Set the potato shells aside.

Serves 4

PER SERVING	
Calories	375
Protein	16 g
Carbohydrates	34 g
Fiber	3 g
Sugar	2 g
Total Fat	19 g
Saturated Fat	10 g
Sodium	507 mg

2 large russet potatoes, washed and dried

2 slices bacon

4 large eggs

½ teaspoon plus a pinch of salt

¼ teaspoon plus a pinch of freshly ground black pepper

2 teaspoons unsalted butter

½ cup sour cream

2 ounces sharp Cheddar cheese, shredded (about ½ cup)

2 tablespoons finely chopped fresh chives, for serving

7 Mash the potato flesh with a fork and stir in the sour cream, ½ teaspoon of salt, and ¼ teaspoon of pepper. Fold the scrambled eggs into the mash.

8 Spoon a quarter of the mixture into each of the potato shells. Crumble the bacon and sprinkle it evenly over the potato halves, then top each with 2 tablespoons of the Cheddar cheese.

9 Bake until the cheese is melted, 2 to 3 minutes. Top each potato half with chives and serve immediately.

SWEET POTATO HASH

A good hash reminds me of Sunday brunches during college with friends at our local diner, served with clunky ceramic mugs of bottomless coffee. The difference between this particular hash and the ones I once ordered is that mine has about half the calories (I use a lot less butter and oil). Feta is lighter and fresher-tasting than the Cheddar I used to go for, and its saltiness is delicious with the sweet potatoes.

_____

1 Preheat the oven to 400°F.

2 On a large rimmed baking sheet, toss the sweet potatoes with the oil, spread them in a single layer, and season with the salt. Roast, stirring halfway, until the potatoes are lightly browned and can easily be pierced with a fork, about 40 minutes. Remove the potatoes from the oven, set aside, and keep the oven on.

3 In a large cast-iron skillet set over medium-high heat, cook the bacon until crisp, 4 to 6 minutes. Transfer the bacon to a paper towel–lined plate. Drain all but 1 tablespoon of the rendered bacon fat from the pan and set the pan over medium heat. Add the onion and bell pepper and cook, stirring occasionally, until softened, 5 to 7 minutes. Add the garlic and cook, stirring constantly, until fragrant, about 30 seconds. Add the potatoes, cumin, chili powder, paprika, and cayenne, and cook, stirring and scraping up any crispy bits, until the potatoes brown further, 2 to 3 minutes.

4 Return the bacon to the pan and stir. Make 4 shallow wells in the hash and crack one egg into each well.

5 Transfer to the oven and bake until the eggs are set but the yolks are still runny, about 6 minutes. Scatter the feta cheese over top of the eggs and bake for 2 more minutes. Garnish with the cilantro and serve immediately.

Serves 4

PER SERVING	
Calories	369
Protein	16 g
Carbohydrates	31 g
Fiber	4 g
Sugar	14 g
Total Fat	20 g
Saturated Fat	8 g
Sodium	861 mg

1½ pounds sweet potatoes, peeled and cut into ½-inch pieces (about 4 cups)

2 teaspoons extra-virgin olive oil

½ teaspoon salt

½ pound (about 8 slices) bacon, chopped

½ large yellow onion, cut into ½-inch pieces (about 1¼ cups)

1 medium green bell pepper, seeded, ribs removed, and cut into ½-inch pieces (about 1½ cups)

2 garlic cloves, minced

1 teaspoon ground cumin

½ teaspoon chili powder

½ teaspoon smoked paprika

Pinch of cayenne pepper

4 large eggs

3 ounces feta cheese, crumbled (about ¾ cup)

Fresh cilantro, for garnish

Lunchtime

CHOPPED SALAD WITH SPICED CHICKPEAS
& TARRAGON-TAHINI DRESSING, *page 48*

CHOPPED SALAD WITH
SPICED CHICKPEAS &
TARRAGON-TAHINI DRESSING   48

ITALIAN SALAD   50

RIBOLLITA   53

LOADED BLACK BEAN
BURGERS   54

ASIAN CHICKEN SALAD   57

TUNA AND ORZO SALAD
WITH PARMESAN & BASIL   58

SWEET POTATO CURRY   61

BAGEL & LOX SALAD   64

THE ULTIMATE BEEF CHILI   66

PETITE LASAGNAS   70

BAKED BUFFALO CHICKEN
EGG ROLLS   72

UPDATED WALDORF
SALAD CUPS   75

CHOPPED SALAD WITH
SPICED CHICKPEAS &
TARRAGON-TAHINI DRESSING

You really have to try tahini. A paste made from ground sesame seeds, it's what makes hummus delicious and this salad irresistible. It's carried by most grocery stores these days, but if you can't find it, check online. The Internet has everything. Don't skip the chickpeas here. The warm spices make them unique enough that you'll fall in love instantly. I'd suggest making a double batch of them so you can have some for snacking.

1   For the dressing, in a small bowl, whisk together the tahini, lemon juice, and 2 tablespoons of water. Whisk in the garlic, tarragon, and salt.

2   For the salad, in a large bowl, toss together the romaine, cucumber, tomatoes, olives, onion, and parsley.

3   To serve, divide the salad among four serving bowls. Top each with a quarter of the feta cheese, a quarter of the chickpeas, and 2 tablespoons of the dressing.

Serves 4

PER SERVING	
Calories	392
Protein	18 g
Carbohydrates	49 g
Fiber	15 g
Sugar	6 g
Total Fat	20 g
Saturated Fat	4 g
Sodium	824 mg

Dressing

3 tablespoons tahini

2 tablespoons fresh lemon juice

1 garlic clove, minced

1 tablespoon finely chopped fresh tarragon

Pinch of salt

Salad

2 romaine lettuce hearts, chopped (about 6 cups)

1 medium cucumber, peeled, halved lengthwise, seeded, and chopped into 1/2-inch pieces (about 1 1/4 cups)

1 pint grape tomatoes, halved

1/3 cup chopped pitted kalamata olives

1/2 cup thinly sliced red onion

1/2 cup packed chopped fresh flat-leaf parsley

3 ounces feta cheese, crumbled (about 3/4 cup)

Spiced Chickpeas (recipe follows)

PER SERVING	
Calories	196
Protein	11 g
Carbohydrates	35 g
Fiber	12 g
Sugar	0 g
Total Fat	6 g
Saturated Fat	0 g
Sodium	543 mg

Spiced Chickpeas
Makes 3½ cups; serves 4

1 teaspoon ground cardamom

½ teaspoon ground cinnamon

1½ teaspoons allspice

1 teaspoon ground cumin

Generous pinch of cayenne pepper

¼ teaspoon salt

2 15-ounce cans chickpeas, rinsed and drained

2 teaspoons olive oil

---

1   In a small bowl, combine the cardamom, cinnamon, allspice, cumin, cayenne, and salt.

2   Pat the chickpeas dry with paper towels. Put them in a gallon-size resealable plastic bag with 1 teaspoon of the olive oil. Seal the bag and shake to coat the chickpeas with the oil. Add the spice mixture, reseal the bag, and shake to coat the chickpeas with the spices.

3   In a 12-inch nonstick skillet, heat the remaining 1 teaspoon of oil over medium-high heat. Add the chickpeas and sauté, shaking the pan occasionally, until they are browned and crispy, about 5 minutes. Serve hot.

4   Let any leftovers cool, and store them in an airtight container in the refrigerator for up to 1 week. Reheat in the microwave for 45 seconds to 1 minute or in a dry skillet over medium heat until warm.

ITALIAN SALAD

In high school I worked at a little pizzeria, and after some of my shifts I'd order a cold Italian sub. Even now, I can almost feel myself eating it, sitting in one of the worn yellow booths—the sandwich piled high with sliced Italian meats and Provolone and topped with a handful of shredded iceberg lettuce, pepperoncini, and a quick drizzle of oil and vinegar. It was perfect.

   This salad is a deconstructed version of that sub. It has all the fixins', down to crisp iceberg and a simple homemade Italian dressing. In salad form, with a moderate amount of meat and cheese, this is a much healthier rendition of the deli classic.

_____

1 For the vinaigrette, in a small bowl, whisk together the oil, vinegar, honey, garlic, oregano, salt, and pepper.

2 For the salad, divide the salami into four even stacks on a clean work surface. Divide the ham and then the Provolone among the four stacks. Starting at the short end of one of the stacks, roll the meat and cheese into a log and then slice the log into ½-inch pinwheels. Repeat with the remaining three stacks.

3 In a large bowl, combine the iceberg, romaine, onions, bell peppers, tomatoes, and pepperoncini. Add the vinaigrette and toss to coat.

4 Divide the salad among 4 plates, top each with a quarter of the meat-and-cheese pinwheels, and serve.

Serves 4

PER SERVING	
Calories	279
Protein	15 g
Carbohydrates	12 g
Fiber	3 g
Sugar	6 g
Total Fat	19 g
Saturated Fat	4 g
Sodium	1135 mg

Vinaigrette

3 tablespoons extra-virgin olive oil

3 tablespoons red wine vinegar

1 teaspoon honey

1 garlic clove, minced

1 teaspoon dried oregano

⅛ teaspoon salt

¼ teaspoon freshly ground black pepper

Salad

4 ounces sliced Genoa salami

4 ounces sliced baked ham

4 ounces sliced Provolone

1 large head of iceberg lettuce, finely shredded (about 8 cups)

1 romaine lettuce heart, chopped

½ large white onion, thinly sliced (¾ cup)

1 large green bell pepper, seeded and thinly sliced (about 1¼ cups)

3 Roma tomatoes, thinly sliced (about 1½ cups)

¼ cup pickled pepperoncini, chopped

RIBOLLITA

There were so many years when I couldn't begin to imagine eating soup as a meal. Unless it was a thick chili or a hearty beef stew, I was curious as to how anyone could feel satisfied after eating a bowl of hot broth.

And then, just after I moved to Manhattan in the winter of 2012, with a storm gusting outside, I felt a chill in my bones that could only be cured with, well, soup. I surprised myself with how much I enjoyed this classic Tuscan soup. It's rich, savory, and interesting enough to fulfill any craving—and as a bonus, it's so darn good for you. If this could convert a non-soup person like me, just think about how delicious it will be for the soup lovers of the world.

---

1 Place the beans in a large pot and fill with enough cold water to cover the beans by 1 inch. Cover and set the beans in the refrigerator to soak for at least 4 hours and up to overnight. Drain the beans and refill the pot with cold water. Bring to a boil over medium-high heat, reduce the heat to low, and simmer until the beans are tender, about 1½ hours. Drain the beans and transfer them to a large bowl.

2 In a large pot, heat the oil over medium heat. Add the onions, carrots, and celery, and stir to coat the vegetables in the oil. Cook, stirring occasionally, until the vegetables are beginning to soften, 12 to 15 minutes.

3 Add the garlic and cook, stirring constantly, until fragrant, about 30 seconds. Add the tomatoes, broth, bay leaf, sage, thyme, and black pepper; increase the heat to medium-high and bring to a boil. Add the beans and kale, cover the pot, reduce the heat to low, and simmer for 25 minutes. Uncover, stir in the bread, and simmer for 10 more minutes.

4 Ladle the soup into bowls and top each with 1 tablespoon of the Parmesan cheese.

Serves 8 (serving size: about 2 cups)

PER SERVING	
Calories	277
Protein	15 g
Carbohydrates	41 g
Fiber	11 g
Sugar	5 g
Total Fat	8 g
Saturated Fat	2 g
Sodium	672 mg

½ pound dried cannellini beans, rinsed and drained

3 tablespoons extra-virgin olive oil

1 medium yellow onion, chopped (about 1 cup)

2 medium carrots, chopped (about 1¼ cups)

2 celery stalks, chopped (about 1¼ cups)

4 garlic cloves, minced

1 15-ounce can crushed tomatoes

2 quarts (8 cups) low-sodium chicken broth

1 bay leaf

2 fresh sage leaves

2 sprigs fresh thyme leaves

½ teaspoon freshly ground black pepper

1 pound lacinato (Tuscan) kale, leaves chopped (about 6 cups)

8 slices day-old crusty whole-grain bread, torn into 1-inch pieces (about 4 cups)

½ cup grated Parmesan cheese

LOADED BLACK BEAN BURGERS

I've gone through several periods in the past eight years or so in which I've dabbled in vegetarian and vegan diets. In the end, though I'd return to eating meat, I'd always have expanded the range of what I ate and what I cooked. I'd have tried new and exotic vegetables and experimented with recipes I never would have considered before. These black bean burgers were one of the happiest creations to come out of my most recent period of vegetarianism. They're packed with flavor and satisfy a craving for a regular burger, but with fewer calories and a lot more nutrients.

Makes 4; serves 4

PER SERVING	
Calories	317
Protein	14 g
Carbohydrates	53 g
Fiber	12 g
Sugar	7 g
Total Fat	8 g
Saturated Fat	1 g
Sodium	734 mg

1 In the bowl of a food processor, combine the scallions, carrots, bell pepper, and cilantro, and pulse until the vegetables are finely chopped, 2 or 3 pulses. Transfer the veggies to a large bowl.

2 Put the beans in the food processor and pulse until finely chopped, 2 or 3 pulses. Add the black beans to the bowl.

3 Put the oats in the food processor and pulse until finely ground. Transfer the oats to the bowl and add the garlic powder, cumin, chili powder, cayenne, salt, ketchup, and egg. Mix well and form into 4 patties.

4 In a 12-inch nonstick skillet set over medium-high heat, heat 1½ teaspoons of the oil. Add 2 of the patties and cook until crisp on one side, about 4 minutes. Carefully flip and cook until the second side is crisp, about 4 minutes more. Transfer to a warm plate. Add the remaining 1½ teaspoons of oil to the skillet and repeat the cooking process with the remaining 2 patties.

2 scallions, white and light-green parts, cut in half

2 large carrots, cut into a few pieces (about 1 cup)

½ medium red bell pepper, seeded, ribs removed, and cut into a few pieces (about ⅔ cup)

¼ cup packed fresh cilantro

1 15-ounce can black beans, rinsed and drained

½ cup quick-cooking oats

½ teaspoon garlic powder

1 teaspoon ground cumin

1 teaspoon chili powder

Pinch of cayenne pepper

½ teaspoon salt

1 tablespoon ketchup

1 large egg

3 teaspoons extra-virgin olive oil

4 whole-wheat hamburger buns, split

4 leaves of romaine lettuce

1 Roma tomato, sliced

1 small red onion, thinly sliced

5   To serve, put the hamburger buns on a clean work surface, place a patty on each of the 4 bottom halves, and layer each with a romaine leaf, a fourth of the tomato slices, a few red onion rings, and the top halves of the buns.

6   The cooked, cooled patties will keep in an airtight container in the refrigerator for up to 5 days. To freeze, put the patties on a parchment paper–lined baking sheet and freeze until completely firm, about 3 hours. Transfer the frozen patties to a large resealable plastic bag and freeze for up to 3 months.

ASIAN CHICKEN SALAD

The first salad that I really fell in love with was the Chinese Chicken
Salad at the Cheesecake Factory. Maybe it was the crisp wontons and
almonds. It could have been the Chinese plum dressing. Or the fact
that the salad was massive. Regardless, it was filling and packed with
flavor—not at all what I'd grown to consider a salad to be. This dish
is a tribute to the salad that made me love salads. Its proportions
are more reasonable, the dressing is lighter and made with peanut
butter, and a few added peanuts lend saltiness and crunch instead of
fried wontons.

1   For the dressing, in a small bowl, whisk together the peanut
    butter, honey, soy sauce, lime juice, and cayenne until smooth.

2   For the salad, season the chicken breasts with the salt
    and pepper. In a 12-inch nonstick skillet, heat the oil over
    medium-high heat. Add the chicken and cook until golden
    brown and cooked through, about 8 minutes per side. Transfer
    to a plate and let cool before slicing into thin strips.

3   In a large bowl, toss the romaine, cabbage, carrots, and
    scallions. Add the sliced chicken, drizzle the dressing over the
    top, and toss gently to coat.

4   To serve, divide the salad among 4 plates or bowls, sprinkle
    with the chopped peanuts, and garnish with the lime quarters.

Serves 4

PER SERVING	
Calories	466
Protein	43 g
Carbohydrates	25 g
Fiber	5 g
Sugar	16 g
Total Fat	23 g
Saturated Fat	4 g
Sodium	452 mg

Dressing

¼ cup creamy natural
   peanut butter
2 tablespoons honey
1 tablespoon low-sodium
   soy sauce
Juice of half a lime
Pinch of cayenne pepper

Salad

1 pound boneless skinless
   chicken breasts
¼ teaspoon salt
¼ teaspoon freshly ground
   black pepper
2 teaspoons extra-virgin olive oil
2 romaine lettuce hearts,
   chopped (about 6 cups)
2 cups finely shredded red
   cabbage (about ¼ head)
2 large carrots, cut into
   matchsticks (about 1 cup)
3 scallions, white and light-green
   parts, chopped (about 1 cup)
½ cup chopped unsalted peanuts
1 lime, quartered, for serving

TUNA AND ORZO SALAD
WITH PARMESAN & BASIL

Tuna has always been a lunch staple of mine. Next to peanut butter, it's just about the most convenient thing around. This ultra-flavorful tuna salad is a departure from the traditional mayo-based ones. It's bright thanks to a lemony vinaigrette, and the white beans add bulk and substance.

---

1 Cook the orzo according to the package directions. Drain and let cool slightly.

2 In a small bowl, whisk together the lemon juice, garlic, honey, salt, pepper, and oil.

3 In a large bowl, combine the warm orzo with the spinach and stir to allow the spinach to wilt slightly. Add the beans, tuna, red onion, celery, tomatoes, and basil. Pour the vinaigrette over the orzo mixture and toss to coat. Stir in the Parmesan cheese.

4 Serve the salad warm, at room temperature, or even chilled. The salad will keep in an airtight container in the refrigerator for 5 days.

Serves 6

PER SERVING	
Calories	435
Protein	21 g
Carbohydrates	55 g
Fiber	7 g
Sugar	6 g
Total Fat	16 g
Saturated Fat	5 g
Sodium	486 mg

1½ cups dry orzo pasta

¼ cup fresh lemon juice (about 2 lemons)

1 garlic clove, minced

1 tablespoon honey

Pinch of salt

Pinch of freshly ground black pepper

¼ cup extra-virgin olive oil

2½ ounces baby spinach leaves (2 packed cups), roughly chopped

1 15-ounce can cannellini beans, rinsed and drained

1 5-ounce can solid white tuna, drained and flaked

½ small red onion, finely chopped (about ½ cup)

1 stalk celery, chopped (about ⅔ cup)

½ cup grape tomatoes, halved

2 tablespoons finely chopped fresh basil leaves

¾ cup coarsely grated Parmesan cheese

SWEET POTATO CURRY

A good curry-infused coconut sauce can get me to eat just about anything. Here, it makes eating a heaping bowlful of chickpeas and vegetables an absolute dream. In making the sauce, I like to add just ⅓ cup of full-fat coconut milk rather than using light coconut milk, as most lighter curry recipes call for, because it gives the sauce richness, a little body, and a whole lot of creaminess. (I always prefer to add a little bit of the good stuff than more of a watered-down version.)

Serves 4

PER SERVING	
Calories	397
Protein	15 g
Carbohydrates	59 g
Fiber	17 g
Sugar	15 g
Total Fat	16 g
Saturated Fat	6 g
Sodium	591 mg

1   In a 12-inch nonstick skillet with a tight-fitting lid, heat 1 tablespoon of the oil over medium-high heat. Add the onion and sweet potato and cook, stirring occasionally, until the onion is browned and the potato begins to soften, about 10 minutes, turning down the heat if needed to prevent burning.

2   Reduce the heat to medium, push the potato and onion to the sides of the pan, and add the remaining 1 tablespoon of oil along with the garlic, jalapeño, ginger, and tomato paste, and cook, stirring constantly, until fragrant, about 30 seconds. Stir in the curry powder, coriander, cardamom, cinnamon, salt, and pepper. Add the cauliflower and cook, stirring constantly, until all the florets are coated, about 1 minute.

3   Add the tomato sauce and chickpeas and 1 cup of water and bring to a boil. Cover, reduce the heat to low, and simmer, stirring occasionally, until the vegetables are tender, about 12 to 15 minutes. Stir in the peas and coconut milk and cook for 2 more minutes. Stir in the cilantro, divide among four bowls, and serve immediately. Leftover curry will keep in an airtight container in the refrigerator for 4 days.

2 tablespoons canola oil

1 large yellow onion, chopped

1 large sweet potato, peeled and cut into ½-inch pieces (about 2 cups)

3 garlic cloves, minced

½ jalapeño, seeded and finely chopped (about 1 tablespoon)

1 tablespoon finely chopped fresh ginger

1 tablespoon tomato paste

2 tablespoons curry powder

1 teaspoon ground coriander

¼ teaspoon ground cardamom

¼ teaspoon ground cinnamon

½ teaspoon salt

¼ teaspoon freshly ground black pepper

½ large head cauliflower, cut into 1-inch florets (about 3 cups)

1 15-ounce can tomato sauce

1 15-ounce can chickpeas, rinsed and drained

2 cups frozen green peas

⅓ cup full-fat coconut milk

¼ cup chopped fresh cilantro

FINDING POWER IN LUNCH

* ❊ *

We ordered out for lunch. That was standard, or so I learned the first week.
"Anything you want, up to twelve dollars," Lori told me.

"Really?"

"Really. Production pays for lunch." She didn't have to say another word before I had ordered every dollar's worth in enchiladas and chips and salsa.

In the beginning, it was just one little perk of working in film—trying all these fabulous restaurants and cafés in whatever new city we were in and having it paid for. We found the most delicious spots, those holes-in-the-wall that only locals know. I loved it. But as someone who was trying to maintain a one-hundred-plus-pound weight loss, ordering out for lunch every day was turning from perk to problem.

This job—a production assistant job on films all around the Northeast—was my first after I graduated from college. I moved from Boston to Philadelphia to one sleepy little town in Connecticut in just two years' time, not entirely knowing what I wanted to do with my life. The job was a dream for a few years, but moving around, living like a nomad, eating out—it had a way of making me feel I was slipping away from the healthy life I'd worked hard to create. Lunch became a daily indulgence. And the calories alone weren't the challenge. Eating an order of pad thai at lunch also had a way of making me feel I'd blown all my good intentions by noon. *Should we get cookies later?* I'd wonder.

I could feel myself backsliding. *What's happening to me?* It felt like old habits reemerging—like the old days when a heavy lunch would lead to a big dinner and an even bigger dessert. *I've got to get a grip.*

For one month, I decided to order salads. Thai, Italian, Mexican—wherever we ordered, I found a salad. Two weeks into this decision, I noticed that I had more energy. I wasn't experiencing the four-o'clock sleepies the way I did when I'd get a huge sandwich. Whatever fear I may have had of getting bored with the salad options had proved to be unnecessary.

Before I knew it, the month had passed, and I surprised myself when I decided to keep going. I began bringing ones I made at home, borrowing inspiration from all the restaurant creations I'd tried—Greek salads with chicken, spiced chickpeas, feta, and hummus; Thai beef salads; taco salads with homemade guacamole;

caprese salads with spinach, fresh mozzarella, and basil. Day in and day out, I was no longer struggling with the constant temptation of what to order; I wasn't fighting myself or testing my willpower. It was salad—plain and simple. And there was comfort in the simple routine of it. I loved knowing that, no matter what else happened in my day as far as food choices went, at least lunch was wholesome.

It has been five years now since those film days, and I still make salads for lunch. I've kept that routine—not every day, but most—because salad, to me, is light, fresh, and easy. Making salad my standard lunch fare—and not testing my willpower every day at noon, means I can use my energy on other things I love, like writing, going to the movies, and planning dinner dates with friends. It's my way of recommitting to the vibrant, healthy life that I want to live. Every day.

BAGEL & LOX SALAD

For me, there are few things as deeply satisfying as a well-toasted pumpernickel bagel with a thick schmear of cream cheese and a few thin slices of lox. I'll have one every now and again, but for the other times when the craving hits, I make this salad. It calls for all of those delicious ingredients but combines them in a fun new way—and with a lot smaller hit to your waistline. The pumpernickel crisps are an especially tasty addition—just a slight nod to the bagel without so many carbs—and I season them with za'atar, a Middle Eastern herb blend that's full of flavor. Fellow bagel-and-lox lovers, you'll adore this!

1   For the dressing, in a small bowl, whisk together the yogurt, oil, parsley, dill, lemon juice, lemon zest, garlic powder, salt, and pepper. Cover and refrigerate while you assemble the rest of the salad.

2   Preheat the oven to 425°F.

3   For the crisps, lay the bread on a clean work surface and, using a rolling pin, flatten each slice to a ¼-inch thickness. In a small bowl, combine the oregano, basil, thyme, garlic powder, salt, and pepper.

4   Put the oil in a separate small bowl and, using a pastry brush, lightly brush both sides of each slice of bread evenly with oil. Put the bread on a wire rack on top of a baking sheet and season with the herb-and-spice mix. Bake until crisp, 6 to 8 minutes. Let cool completely.

Serves 4

PER SERVING	
Calories	271
Protein	16 g
Carbohydrates	20 g
Fiber	4 g
Sugar	5 g
Total Fat	15 g
Saturated Fat	2 g
Sodium	1517 mg

Dressing

¼ cup plain 2% Greek yogurt

2 tablespoons extra-virgin olive oil

1 teaspoon finely chopped fresh flat-leaf parsley

1 teaspoon chopped fresh dill

1 tablespoon fresh lemon juice

½ teaspoon freshly grated lemon zest

⅛ teaspoon garlic powder

Pinch of salt

Pinch of freshly ground black pepper

Pumpernickel Crisps

4 slices pumpernickel bread

1 teaspoon dried oregano

1 teaspoon dried basil

1 teaspoon dried thyme

⅛ teaspoon garlic powder

¼ teaspoon salt

¼ teaspoon freshly ground black pepper

1 tablespoon extra-virgin olive oil

5   For the salad, in a large bowl, toss the arugula, butter lettuce, cucumber, and red onion. Divide the salad evenly among 4 plates and lay the salmon slices on top of each. Sprinkle 1 teaspoon of the capers over each, and drizzle the dressing evenly over the top of each plate. Roughly break apart 1 pumpernickel crisp over each salad and serve.

Salad

5 ounces arugula

1 small head of butter lettuce or Bibb lettuce, chopped (about 6 cups)

1 large English cucumber, thinly sliced (about 1½ cups)

½ medium red onion, very thinly sliced (about ⅔ cup)

8 ounces smoked salmon, thinly sliced

4 teaspoons capers, rinsed and drained

THE ULTIMATE BEEF CHILI

This chunky beef chili is hands-down my favorite. It's intense and flavorful with just the right amount of spice to warm you up in fall and winter. I like to add a bottle of dark beer because it gives the dish a little bit of richness, but don't worry about it imparting any detectable alcohol flavor.

_____

1   In a large stockpot, cook the bacon over medium-high heat until crisp, 4 to 5 minutes. Transfer to a paper towel–lined plate to drain. Add the ground beef to the pot and sauté, breaking it up with a rubber spatula, until browned, about 6 minutes. Transfer the beef to a plate.

2   Add the onion and bell pepper to the pot and cook, stirring frequently, until softened and faintly golden, about 5 minutes. Add the garlic and cook, stirring constantly, until fragrant, about 30 seconds. Stir in the chili powder, cumin, paprika, tomato paste, and salt. Add the beer, tomatoes, chipotle chile, broth, and the black and kidney beans. Crumble the cooked bacon into the pot, and add the cooked ground beef. Increase the heat and bring to a boil, reduce the heat to low, and simmer for at least 1 hour.

3   Divide the chili among 6 bowls and top each with cilantro, red onion, 2 tablespoons of Cheddar cheese, and sour cream, if desired.

Makes 9 cups; serves 6

PER SERVING	
Calories	437
Protein	31 g
Carbohydrates	40 g
Fiber	12 g
Sugar	3 g
Total Fat	17 g
Saturated Fat	8 g
Sodium	925 mg

2 slices bacon

1 pound ground sirloin (90% lean)

1 medium onion, chopped

1 medium green bell pepper, seeded and chopped

3 garlic cloves, minced

2 tablespoons chili powder

2 tablespoons ground cumin

2 teaspoons paprika

2 tablespoons tomato paste

¼ teaspoon salt

1 12-ounce bottle amber beer

1 28-ounce can crushed tomatoes

1 chipotle chile in adobo (from a can), finely chopped

1½ cups low-sodium chicken broth

1 15-ounce can black beans, rinsed and drained

1 15-ounce can kidney beans, rinsed and drained

1 cup chopped fresh cilantro

Chopped red onion (optional)

3 ounces Cheddar cheese, shredded (about ¾ cup)

Sour cream (optional)

PETITE LASAGNAS

My Nana Mitchell made a mean lasagna. Sure, maybe there were times when she froze it for several years before reheating it and serving the especially freezer-burned corner piece to me, but I'm telling you, it was damn good when it was fresh.

With everything you love about a cheesy, red sauce–sputtering pan of lasagna, these hassle-free mini cups taste like the real deal. An added bonus is that they're innately portion controlled. While I love serving them as an appetizer—no one expects them!—you can also serve a few alongside a big salad as a main course. They freeze well, too, but just for a couple of months (not years!). Serve these cuties with a side of Perfect Roasted Broccoli (page 100).

Note that this recipe uses wonton wrappers, which are smaller than the egg roll wrappers used in the Baked Buffalo Chicken Egg Rolls (page 72).

Makes 12; serves 6

PER SERVING	
Calories	374
Protein	34 g
Carbohydrates	33 g
Fiber	3 g
Sugar	2 g
Total Fat	12 g
Saturated Fat	6 g
Sodium	670 mg

2 teaspoons extra-virgin olive oil

12 ounces ground turkey breast

1 small yellow onion, finely chopped (about 1 cup)

½ cup finely chopped mushrooms

½ teaspoon salt

½ teaspoon freshly ground black pepper

2 garlic cloves, minced

1 15-ounce can crushed tomatoes or tomato sauce

3 teaspoons dried oregano

1½ cups part-skim ricotta cheese

2 teaspoons dried basil

24 square (3½-inch) wonton wrappers

4 ounces shredded mozzarella cheese (about 1 cup)

1 Preheat the oven to 350°F.

2 In a 12-inch nonstick skillet, heat the oil over medium-high heat. Add the turkey, onion, mushrooms, ¼ teaspoon of the salt, and ¼ teaspoon of the pepper, and sauté, breaking up the meat with a rubber spatula, until the turkey is cooked through, 7 to 10 minutes.

3 Add the garlic and cook, stirring constantly, until fragrant, about 30 seconds. Add the tomatoes and 2 teaspoons of the oregano and bring the mixture to a simmer. Reduce the heat to medium-low and cook for 10 minutes. Remove the pan from the heat and set aside.

4 In a medium bowl, combine the ricotta, the remaining ¼ teaspoon of the salt, the remaining ¼ teaspoon of the pepper, the remaining 1 teaspoon of the oregano, and the basil.

5   Spray a standard 12-cup muffin tin with nonstick cooking spray. Put 1 wonton wrapper in the bottom of each of the 12 cups, pressing firmly into the bottom of the cup and up the sides. Divide half of the ricotta mixture among the 12 muffin cups. Divide half of the turkey tomato sauce evenly over each of the ricotta-filled cups. Sprinkle each with 2 teaspoons of the mozzarella cheese. Gently press another wonton wrapper on top. Repeat the layering process with the remaining ingredients.

6   Bake until the lasagnas are hot in the centers and the cheese has melted, 12 to 15 minutes. Transfer to a wire rack and let cool for 5 minutes in the pan before serving.

BAKED BUFFALO CHICKEN
EGG ROLLS

As unromantic as it might sound, buffalo chicken reminds me of my longtime boyfriend Daniel—and of falling in love. When we first started dating years ago, we used any money we could scrounge up on takeout pizzas, calzones, and subs smothered in hot sauce and cool, creamy blue cheese dressing. Because their associated memories are so important, I can't forever say good-bye to these flavors, so I came up with a lighter way to have them. Crunchy baked egg roll wrappers take the place of the fried chicken, and just a touch of that creamy dressing goes a long way.

Makes 12; serves 4

PER SERVING

Calories	351
Protein	32 g
Carbohydrates	16 g
Fiber	1 g
Sugar	2 g
Total Fat	16 g
Saturated Fat	6 g
Sodium	995 mg

2 medium boneless skinless chicken breasts (about 12 ounces total)

⅓ cup Frank's RedHot Sauce

12 egg roll wrappers (roughly 4 square inches each)

1 cup broccoli slaw or coleslaw mix

3 ounces blue cheese, crumbled (about ¾ cup)

½ cup light blue cheese dressing, for serving (I like Ken's Steak House Lite Chunky Blue Cheese)

1   Put the chicken in a small saucepan and fill with enough water to cover. Set the pan over medium-high heat and bring to a boil. Reduce the heat to medium-low and simmer until the chicken is cooked through, about 12 minutes. Drain and let cool. Using two forks, shred the chicken and put it into a small bowl. Add the hot sauce and stir well.

2   Preheat the oven to 400°F.

3   Lay the egg roll wrappers on a clean work surface. Put about 1 tablespoon of the broccoli slaw toward the bottom-right corner of one of the wrappers. Put 2 tablespoons chicken on the slaw and top with 1 tablespoon of the blue cheese. Fold the bottom-right corner over the stuffing, so the tip of the corner points to the center of the wrapper. Fold in the bottom-left corner to form an envelope. Roll the wrap away from you one time. Moisten the top-left corner with water and then seal the roll. Put the roll on a wire rack set on top of a rimmed baking sheet that has been sprayed with nonstick cooking spray. Repeat with the remaining ingredients.

4   Spray the rolls evenly with nonstick cooking spray and bake until they are crisp and light golden brown, 12 to 15 minutes. Serve hot, with blue cheese dressing for dipping.

UPDATED WALDORF SALAD CUPS

About two years ago, my mom was at a point where she felt her size was becoming burdensome. She wanted to lose weight, and she asked me to help her. She even asked me to blog about it. "It'll give me some accountability, Andrea—knowing that I have to share my progress. And I just know there are other women out there who are in the same boat." I was sure I was going to go to hell for putting my mom on a diet, but, well, here goes nothing.

I made her a meal plan. The hard part, in the beginning, was that Mom was an incredibly picky eater. So when I wanted to get her to start including salads in her life—ones without lots of heavy dressings—I knew I had to make them interesting. This recipe, with all of the delicious mix-ins, did the trick, and the lettuce wraps gave her the sense that she was eating a sandwich. Mom loved it. And what she loved even more? Four months after we'd started the diet, she was down thirty pounds.

---

1 In a large bowl, whisk together the oil, vinegar, honey, salt, and pepper. Add the chicken, celery, parsley, cabbage, pear, and Gorgonzola, and toss well to coat all ingredients in the dressing. Cover the bowl and refrigerate for 30 minutes.

2 To serve, place 2 butter lettuce leaves on each of 4 plates and divide the salad among the lettuce cups.

Serves 4

PER SERVING	
Calories	365
Protein	26 g
Carbohydrates	15 g
Fiber	2 g
Sugar	11 g
Total Fat	22 g
Saturated Fat	8 g
Sodium	364 mg

3 tablespoons extra-virgin olive oil

3 tablespoons apple cider vinegar

1 tablespoon plus 1 teaspoon honey

Pinch of salt

Pinch of freshly ground black pepper

2 cups chopped (¼-inch pieces) cooked boneless skinless chicken breast (about 12 ounces)

2 celery stalks, thinly sliced on the bias (about 1¼ cups)

¼ cup packed chopped fresh flat-leaf parsley

1 cup finely shredded red cabbage

1 large pear, halved, cored, and chopped into ¼-inch pieces (I like Bosc or Anjou pears)

3 ounces Gorgonzola cheese, crumbled (¾ cup)

8 butter lettuce leaves

Vegetables & Sides

GREEK SALSA, *page 80*

GREEK SALSA 80

BUTTERNUT SQUASH SALAD
WITH KALE & POMEGRANATE 81

KALE CHIPS 83

ARUGULA WITH ORANGE
SEGMENTS, SPICED
WALNUTS & GOAT CHEESE 84

SHREDDED BRUSSELS
SPROUTS SALAD WITH
BACON, APPLE &
GORGONZOLA 87

SMASHED ROASTED GARLIC
POTATOES 89

ROASTED CARROTS WITH
HONEY BUTTER 92

MASHED SWEET POTATOES
WITH ORANGE ZEST & BASIL 95

COCONUT CURRY BRUSSELS
SPROUTS 96

CAULIFLOWER WITH BACON 99

PERFECT ROASTED
BROCCOLI 100

SESAME GREEN BEANS 103

GREEK SALSA

I love a good salsa, and this one is refreshingly different. Not only does it use one of my favorite cheeses (feta) and one of my favorite habit-forming substances (pita chips), but it packs a ton of flavor. It's bright, punchy, and just rich enough to leave you feeling satisfied after a few spoonfuls. It's pretty versatile, too; try it on eggs in the morning, with fresh vegetables for a snack, or even on top of grilled chicken to dress up your dinner! A serving of salsa is two heaping tablespoons, but you won't need more than a little bit on each chip because the flavors go a long way!

Makes about 2 cups; serves 12

PER SERVING	
Calories	146
Protein	3 g
Carbohydrates	14 g
Fiber	1 g
Sugar	1 g
Total Fat	9 g
Saturated Fat	2 g
Sodium	347 mg

1 In a large bowl, combine the feta, olives, onion, cucumber, sun-dried tomatoes, mint, and parsley. Add the olive oil, lemon juice, salt, and pepper, and stir well. Cover the bowl and refrigerate for at least 30 minutes and up to 6 hours.

2 Serve the salsa with pita chips for dipping.

3 ounces feta cheese, crumbled (about ¾ cup)

½ cup chopped pitted kalamata olives

⅓ cup finely chopped red onion

½ cup finely chopped English cucumber

4 sun-dried tomatoes packed in olive oil, drained, pressed dry with a paper towel, and finely chopped (about ½ cup)

1 tablespoon finely chopped fresh mint leaves

1 tablespoon finely chopped fresh flat-leaf parsley

2 tablespoons extra-virgin olive oil

2 tablespoons fresh lemon juice

Pinch of salt

¼ teaspoon freshly ground black pepper

1 bag baked pita chips, for serving (I like Stacy's Simply Naked Pita Chips)

BUTTERNUT SQUASH SALAD
WITH KALE & POMEGRANATE

This is my favorite fall salad—a sweet and filling mixture of so many healthy seasonal ingredients. That is, hands down, the best definition of what a salad can be. I love to eat it when the squash is hot from the oven, but it tastes just as great chilled if you want to make it ahead of time and pack it for lunch!

———————

1   For the cider vinaigrette, in a small bowl, whisk together the oil, vinegar, honey, Dijon, cinnamon, and salt.

2   Preheat the oven to 350°F.

3   For the salad, spread the walnuts on a large rimmed baking sheet and toast until fragrant and golden brown, 8 to 10 minutes. Transfer the walnuts to a small bowl.

4   Increase the oven temperature to 425°F.

5   Using the same rimmed baking sheet, toss the squash and oil together. Spread the squash out in a single layer, season with the salt, and roast, stirring halfway, until the squash is browned and can be pierced easily with a fork, about 40 minutes.

6   In a large bowl, toss the kale with the vinaigrette, taking care to coat all the leaves. Add the squash, pomegranate arils, and walnuts and toss well. Divide among 4 plates and serve.

Serves 4

PER SERVING	
Calories	352
Protein	8 g
Carbohydrates	32 g
Fiber	7 g
Sugar	13 g
Total Fat	24 g
Saturated Fat	3 g
Sodium	242 mg

Cider Vinaigrette

3 tablespoons extra-virgin
   olive oil
2 tablespoons apple cider
   vinegar
1 tablespoon plus 1 teaspoon
   honey
2 teaspoons Dijon mustard
¼ teaspoon ground cinnamon
Pinch of salt

Salad

½ cup chopped unsalted
   walnuts
1 1½-pound butternut squash,
   peeled, seeded, and cut into
   ¾-inch pieces (about 8 cups)
1 tablespoon olive oil
¼ teaspoon salt
5 ounces baby kale leaves,
   roughly chopped (about 5 cups
   packed)
½ cup fresh pomegranate arils

KALE CHIPS

Kale is a superfood that's loaded with vitamins and minerals, and just knowing that fact makes me feel good while eating it. But the thing I really love about kale—and loads of other green veggies—is that it fills me up for so few calories. Kale chips provide all the volume I want in my snacks and meals while satisfying my salty, crunchy cravings for potato chips.

Serves 4

PER SERVING	
Calories	72
Protein	4 g
Carbohydrates	8 g
Fiber	4 g
Sugar	3 g
Total Fat	4 g
Saturated Fat	1 g
Sodium	328 mg

6 large kale leaves
1 tablespoon extra-virgin
 olive oil
¼ teaspoon salt
⅛ teaspoon freshly ground black
 pepper

1 Preheat the oven to 350°F.

2 Remove the thick stems from the kale leaves and cut the leaves into 2-inch pieces.

3 In a large bowl, combine the kale pieces and olive oil, tossing well to coat all the leaves.

4 Spread the kale in a single layer on a rimmed baking sheet and bake until crisp and dark around the edges, 10 to 12 minutes.

5 Season with the salt and pepper and serve immediately.

ARUGULA WITH ORANGE SEGMENTS, SPICED WALNUTS & GOAT CHEESE

Often spiced-walnut recipes involve a lot of butter, which means fat and calories. Sure, it tastes good, but is it always necessary? I found that it's not, and that just an egg white, a little sugar, and some warm spices give the nuts a really flavorful coating. Tossed with arugula, orange segments, and fresh goat cheese, these walnuts make a delicious salad that's great next to my Bacon-Wrapped Pork Tenderloin (page 157).

1   For the spiced walnuts, preheat the oven to 325°F. Line a rimmed baking sheet with parchment paper.

2   In a small bowl, combine the sugar, chili powder, allspice, salt, and pepper. In another small bowl, toss the walnuts with the egg white. Using a slotted spoon, transfer the walnuts to the baking sheet, sprinkle the spices over the top, and toss until they are completely coated.

3   Bake, stirring every 5 minutes, until the coating is a deep golden brown, about 25 minutes.

4   Transfer the nuts to a plate and spread in a single layer to cool completely.

5   For the salad, in a large bowl, whisk together the oil, vinegar, preserves, mint, and salt. Add the arugula and toss to coat in the vinaigrette. Add the spiced walnuts, goat cheese, and oranges and toss once more.

6   Divide the salad among 4 plates and serve immediately.

Serves 6

PER SERVING

Calories	260
Protein	9 g
Carbohydrates	18 g
Fiber	3 g
Sugar	14 g
Total Fat	18 g
Saturated Fat	5 g
Sodium	164 mg

Spiced Walnuts

3 tablespoons sugar

¼ teaspoon chili powder

¼ teaspoon allspice

¼ teaspoon salt

¼ teaspoon freshly ground black pepper

½ cup coarsely chopped unsalted walnuts

1 large egg white, lightly beaten

Salad

3 tablespoons extra-virgin olive oil

2 tablespoons balsamic vinegar

2 tablespoons all-fruit raspberry preserves

1 tablespoon finely chopped fresh mint leaves

Pinch of salt

5 ounces baby arugula (5 cups)

3 ounces goat cheese, crumbled (¾ cup)

2 large oranges, segmented

SHREDDED BRUSSELS SPROUTS SALAD WITH BACON, APPLE & GORGONZOLA

I was in the habit of preparing Brussels sprouts only one way—roasting them—when I realized I could cut the cooking time significantly and end up with a fantastic slaw if I simply shredded and lightly sautéed the sprouts. This recipe uses that new and delicious technique: a crisp salad of Brussels, bacon, sweet Granny Smith apple, and pungent Gorgonzola cheese. The flavors play so well together that I never want them to be apart. If you're not wild about Gorgonzola, you can use feta, goat, or another blue cheese with great results.

Serves 4

PER SERVING	
Calories	203
Protein	11 g
Carbohydrates	19 g
Fiber	7 g
Sugar	7 g
Total Fat	11 g
Saturated Fat	6 g
Sodium	608 mg

1½ pounds Brussels sprouts, trimmed (about 4 cups)

4 slices bacon

½ teaspoon salt

¼ teaspoon freshly ground black pepper

1 large Granny Smith apple, peeled, cored, and finely chopped (about 1 cup)

2 ounces Gorgonzola cheese, crumbled (½ cup)

1   Halve the sprouts and thinly slice them into ribbons lengthwise. Rub the slices gently between your fingers to separate the layers and put them into a large bowl.

2   In a 12-inch nonstick skillet set over medium-high heat, cook the bacon until crisp, 5 to 7 minutes. Transfer to a paper towel–lined plate to drain.

3   Pour off all but 1 tablespoon of the rendered bacon fat from the pan and return the pan to medium-high heat. Add the sprouts, salt, and pepper, and cook, stirring frequently, until browned, 4 to 5 minutes.

4   Transfer the sprouts to a large bowl, crumble the bacon on top, and add the apple pieces and cheese. Toss to combine, divide among 4 plates, and serve.

SMASHED ROASTED GARLIC POTATOES

The only other person who loves potatoes as fiercely as I do is my mother. The woman loves them—along with a number of other things, including salted butter, socks that match your outfit, calling 411, and telling me to wear more lipstick. Potatoes are what she's most famous for, other than being the founder and CEO of me. These smashed, garlicky Yukon Golds are not only a tribute to my favorite lady, they're also the perfect side dish. They're crisp and crusty with soft, mashy middles. They'll give you a faint crackling sound upon biting into them that is hard to beat.

Serves 4

PER SERVING	
Calories	170
Protein	3 g
Carbohydrates	28 g
Fiber	5 g
Sugar	0 g
Total Fat	5 g
Saturated Fat	1 g
Sodium	338 mg

1½ pounds small Yukon Gold potatoes (about 8 small potatoes)

4 teaspoons extra-virgin olive oil

½ teaspoon salt

½ teaspoon freshly ground black pepper

3 garlic cloves, minced

2 tablespoons grated Parmesan cheese

1 Preheat the oven to 350°F. Line a large rimmed baking sheet with parchment.

2 Put the potatoes on the baking sheet and bake until tender enough to be easily pierced with a fork, about 45 minutes. Remove the baking sheet from the oven and increase the oven temperature to 450°F.

3 With the potatoes still on the baking sheet, place the bottom of another large baking sheet on top of them and press down to smash them. Be careful not to press too firmly and break the potatoes apart. Remove the top baking sheet and brush both sides of the potatoes evenly with 2 teaspoons of the oil. Season with ¼ teaspoon of the salt and the ½ teaspoon of pepper and sprinkle the garlic over the tops.

4 Roast the potatoes until brown and crisp, about 15 minutes. Remove the pan from the oven, brush the tops of the potatoes with 1 teaspoon of oil, flip them, and brush the other sides with the remaining teaspoon of oil. Season with the remaining ¼ teaspoon of salt.

5 Roast until deep golden brown, about 15 minutes. Sprinkle with the Parmesan and roast for 5 more minutes. Serve hot.

A NEW WAY OF FILLING UP

* ❁ *

What's the first thing you'll eat when you get there?"

By "there," she meant my goal weight. It was a topic we'd talked about for months now, and a question I'd mulled over a thousand times—especially in the moments when I would have sold my kidney for a cheeseburger.

I put my elbows on the table and looked up, searching the air as if considering all the options, when really I was just stalling. I had no idea at this point—not of what I'd eat but of *how* I'd be able to do it. The closer I got to thinness, the more I started to wonder, *Am I going to have to diet for the rest of my life?*

"Pizza, maybe?" I missed pizza.

Kate nodded. "That's what I'd choose."

I wanted to imagine that I'd get to thinness and find pizza waiting at the door, but the tail end of my weight loss brought with it a sense of claustrophobia I wasn't expecting. I wasn't sure I'd be able to stop at one slice of pizza, one square of lasagna. I knew how to lose weight by eating completely healthy . . . but moderation? Not my strong suit. I wanted to be able to enjoy food, to be able to go out to eat and not feel limited to the salads section of the menu. But then I also didn't quite feel safe branching out.

"I'm kind of scared, though," I said to Kate.

"Of what?"

"That I'm never going to be able to have all the foods I used to like again." I pushed the salad around on my plate.

She leaned forward. "Don't be scared of that. Look, it might take time to figure out how to work them in, but you'll prove to yourself that you can. I know you."

I looked at her, sitting across from me in the booth at our favorite café, and for the seven millionth time in our best friendship, I wondered how she managed to eat everything she wanted and still stay thin. It seemed impossible—for her, for me. She picked at her french fries, barely finishing them, and a part of me recognized that before this whole weight loss thing started, I never would have left a fry behind. *Does anyone leave a lone fry?*

She pushed her salad plate away—the one she'd started the meal with—and leaned in. "There's no reason to think the journey just stops when you get there. Maybe you start a new one."

How lucky was I, in seventh grade, to have found Kate?

She was right. When I got there, months later, to that mecca of a goal weight I'd set, I had to start a brand new journey—only this one wasn't about abstinence; it was about moderation.

I did get that pizza. But the first few times I ordered it with friends, I learned the hard way that the slices added up quickly—and didn't fill me up until I'd consumed half a day's worth of calories. From then on, I never ordered pizza without a salad to go with it, and I found that it helped me not only to stop at two slices but to slow down and enjoy those slices even more. When I went home to Massachusetts and had a big Italian dinner with my parents—our Sunday night tradition—it took no time at all for me to realize that, unless I filled half of my plate with roasted vegetables, the penne would become bottomless.

In the end, the more vegetables, fruits, and big leafy salads I introduced, the easier eating in moderation became. They were filling me. They were giving me that volume that I craved, that I was used to—and pairing them with heavier foods started to make perfect sense.

Soon I wasn't just eating vegetables for the sake of fullness; I was learning to love them. At the market, I bought ones I'd never tried before—ones I'd never even heard of—and experimented with different ways of cooking them. I roasted, steamed, mashed, and stir-fried them. I added spices, sauces, and fresh herbs, and the adventurer in me began to feel as excited about broccoli as I did about steak.

Ten years ago, sitting across from Kate, scared of how I'd ever eat the foods I love again, I wouldn't have believed that vegetables would be the answer to helping me eat in moderation. But they were. They are. Ten years ago, I didn't know how anyone could stop at one serving of anything. And here I am, all these years later, finally full.

ROASTED CARROTS WITH HONEY BUTTER

Whenever I travel home to Massachusetts to visit my parents, no matter how long I stay, I inevitably become the cook. And if ever I make roasted carrots, my mom bites her lip and asks, "Do you think we should glaze them?" That's her thing: glazed carrots. And when I say "glazed," I mean a pan of caramel with a carrot or two sliced into it. So I sigh. She says never mind. And I glaze them. Because she's my love, and I do what I can to make her happy. The one way I've been able to mitigate a pan of buttery brown sugar caramel is to create this lighter browned-butter glaze for the carrots. Trust me—I know how it sounds. *Lighter* browned butter? Used as a flavor enhancer more than a foundation, this glaze makes all of us happy.

Serves 4

PER SERVING	
Calories	127
Protein	2 g
Carbohydrates	20 g
Fiber	5 g
Sugar	14 g
Total Fat	5 g
Saturated Fat	2 g
Sodium	344 mg

1½ pounds carrots

2 teaspoons extra-virgin olive oil

½ teaspoon salt

1 tablespoon unsalted butter

1 tablespoon honey

Pinch of freshly ground black pepper

1 Preheat the oven to 425°F.

2 Cut the carrots in half width-wise and then cut them in halves or even quarters length-wise to form long, uniform pieces.

3 On a large rimmed baking sheet, toss the carrots with the oil, spread them out in a single layer, and season with the salt. Roast, stirring halfway, until browned and tender, 35 to 40 minutes.

4 When the carrots are nearly done, in a small nonstick skillet set over medium heat, melt the butter and cook, swirling the pan occasionally, until just faintly golden, about 2 minutes. Remove the pan from the heat and stir in the honey.

5 Transfer the roasted carrots to a large bowl while still hot and pour the honey butter over the top. Toss to coat, season with pepper, and serve immediately.

MASHED SWEET POTATOES
WITH ORANGE ZEST & BASIL

The secret to the best mashed sweet potatoes? Baking instead of boiling. I'm telling you, they're so much better this way, you'll never go back. The natural sugars become more concentrated—almost maple syrupy. I barely have to sweeten this version, but I do like to add new flavors, like orange zest and fragrant basil.

_____

1 Preheat the oven to 400°F.

2 Line a large rimmed baking sheet with aluminum foil. Prick the sweet potatoes all over with a fork and arrange them on the baking sheet. Bake until a fork can be inserted easily into the center of one, flipping halfway, about 45 minutes.

3 Slice each potato in half lengthwise and scoop out the flesh into a large bowl. Add the butter, milk, nutmeg, maple syrup, salt, orange zest, and pepper, and mash thoroughly. Stir in the basil and serve immediately.

Serves 6

PER SERVING	
Calories	157
Protein	2 g
Carbohydrates	29 g
Fiber	3 g
Sugar	12 g
Total Fat	4 g
Saturated Fat	2 g
Sodium	208 mg

2½ pounds sweet potatoes, washed and dried

2 tablespoons unsalted butter

2 tablespoons 2% milk

Pinch of ground nutmeg

1 teaspoon pure maple syrup

½ teaspoon salt

¾ teaspoon freshly grated orange zest

Pinch of freshly ground black pepper

2 teaspoons finely chopped fresh basil leaves

COCONUT CURRY
BRUSSELS SPROUTS

I didn't try Brussels sprouts until I was twenty-five years old. I guess I assumed they were like blond highlights on dark-brown hair—something I was grateful to have narrowly escaped in my teens. And then, once when I was eating at a restaurant, I had them roasted. They were caramelized and crispy, salty yet sweet. I loved them immediately and haven't stopped eating them since.

Roasting Brussels sprouts is *the way* to eat them. For this recipe, I played with two of my favorite flavors: curry and coconut. Both just so happen to pair beautifully together while also enhancing the natural sweetness of the roasted Brussels.

1 Preheat the oven to 400°F.

2 In a large bowl, toss the Brussels sprouts with the coconut oil, curry powder, and salt. Spread the sprouts on a large rimmed baking sheet lined with aluminum foil, cut sides down, and roast until browned and tender, about 25 minutes.

3 Remove the pan from the oven, add the coconut, and stir well. Return the pan to the oven and continue roasting until the coconut is fragrant and beginning to turn a light golden brown, about 5 more minutes. Serve immediately.

Serves 4

PER SERVING	
Calories	144
Protein	7 g
Carbohydrates	20 g
Fiber	8 g
Sugar	5 g
Total Fat	7 g
Saturated Fat	5 g
Sodium	343 mg

2 pounds Brussels sprouts, trimmed and halved (about 6 cups)

1 tablespoon coconut oil

1 teaspoon curry powder

½ teaspoon salt

¼ cup unsweetened coconut flakes

CAULIFLOWER WITH BACON

I'll say it so you don't have to: cauliflower can be bland city. For a long time I wasn't even sure there was a point in trying to love it at all, but then I did what I always do when I'm unsure of how to proceed: I got out the bacon. It makes everything better, and this is no exception. Chopping up two slices—just enough to get the flavor but not plunge into indulgence—tossing the bacon with the florets, and roasting them all together made sure that the cauliflower picked up the salty, rich flavor of the bacon while achieving its own magical caramelization. Here, dear friends, is a way to begin loving cauliflower.

_____

1 Preheat the oven to 425°F.

2 On a large rimmed baking sheet lined with aluminum foil, toss the cauliflower with the oil and garlic, and spread the florets into a single layer. Scatter the bacon pieces around the pan and season with the sugar, salt, and pepper.

3 Roast, stirring halfway, until the cauliflower is browned and tender and the bacon is crisp, about 30 minutes. Serve immediately.

Serves 4

PER SERVING	
Calories	121
Protein	3 g
Carbohydrates	6 g
Fiber	2 g
Sugar	3 g
Total Fat	10 g
Saturated Fat	3 g
Sodium	400 mg

1 head of cauliflower (about 2 pounds), cut into florets (about 6 cups)

1 tablespoon extra-virgin olive oil

2 garlic cloves, minced

2 slices bacon, cut into ½-inch pieces

½ teaspoon sugar

½ teaspoon salt

¼ teaspoon freshly ground black pepper

PERFECT ROASTED BROCCOLI

Serves 4

PER SERVING	
Calories	72
Protein	4 g
Carbohydrates	8 g
Fiber	4 g
Sugar	3 g
Total Fat	4 g
Saturated Fat	1 g
Sodium	328 mg

I'd go so far as to say that broccoli is the best vegetable, but I can't do that to Brussels sprouts. You know how insecure they are. I've done everything with broccoli. Steamed it, sautéed it, fried it, covered it with beaten eggs, and scrambled it in butter and Pecorino Romano cheese to make my grandmother's famous side dish, creatively titled Broccoli and Eggs. And then, two years ago, I roasted it. Ever since, I haven't looked back. The high heat brings out a faint but noticeable sweetness, and that, combined with a good hearty sprinkling of salt and fragrant garlic, is just such a happy thing.

2 pounds broccoli, cut into florets

2 garlic cloves, minced

1 tablespoon extra-virgin olive oil

½ teaspoon salt

1   Preheat the oven to 425°F.

2   In a large bowl, toss the broccoli and garlic with the olive oil. Spread the broccoli and garlic on a large rimmed baking sheet and season evenly with the salt. Roast, stirring halfway, until the broccoli is tender but still crisp and beginning to brown, 25 to 30 minutes.

SESAME GREEN BEANS

Green beans—or string beans, as my family likes to call them—are a staple vegetable in my house. The problem is that they can get boring, fast. Here, I whisked up a quick Asian-style dressing made with warm, smoky toasted sesame oil and honey to add a little excitement to an otherwise ordinary side. A sprinkle of toasted sesame seeds lends the slightest bit of crunch and even dresses the beans up a bit if you're planning to serve them to guests.

_____

1 For the dressing, in a small bowl, whisk together the honey, soy sauce, oil, and garlic.

2 For the green beans, in a small nonstick skillet set over medium heat, toast the sesame seeds, shaking the pan frequently to prevent burning, until lightly golden and fragrant, 1 to 2 minutes.

3 In a large saucepan set over high heat, bring 1 quart water and the salt to a boil. Add the green beans, return the water to a boil, and cook until the beans are bright in color and just tender, about 5 minutes. Drain the beans and transfer them to a large serving bowl. Add the soy dressing and the sesame seeds and toss to coat. Serve immediately.

Serves 4

PER SERVING	
Calories	85
Protein	3 g
Carbohydrates	12 g
Fiber	3 g
Sugar	7 g
Total Fat	4 g
Saturated Fat	0 g
Sodium	174 mg

Dressing

1 tablespoon honey

2 teaspoons low-sodium
   soy sauce

2 teaspoons toasted sesame oil

1 garlic clove, minced

Green Beans

1 tablespoon sesame seeds

1 teaspoon salt

1 pound green beans, trimmed
   (about 4 cups)

Dinnertime

JERK SHRIMP SALAD
WITH MANGO & AVOCADA, *page 109*

JERK SHRIMP SALAD
WITH MANGO & AVOCADO   109

LEMON-HERB FISH
WITH CRISPY OVEN FRIES   110

BROWN SUGAR & CHILI-RUBBED
SALMON WITH AVOCADO CREMA   113

SPICY TOFU STIR-FRY
WITH BOK CHOY   115

HALIBUT BAKED IN PARCHMENT WITH
PISTACHIO MINT PESTO   118

CREAMY FARRO WITH
WHITE BEANS & KALE   122

LIGHTENED-UP PAD THAI
IN UNDER 15 MINUTES   125

SOUTHWESTERN PULLED CHICKEN
WITH CILANTRO LIME SLAW   126

CHICKEN CURRY WITH
GINGER & YOGURT   131

BEEF PUTTANESCA WITH
GARLIC BREAD   133

CHICKEN WITH SUN-DRIED
TOMATOES & FETA   137

LEMON ROASTED CHICKEN
WITH MOROCCAN COUSCOUS   138

141 CHICKEN & MUSHROOMS IN
MUSTARD MARSALA CREAM SAUCE

145 SPAGHETTI WITH BRUSSELS
SPROUTS & PANCETTA CREAM

146 TURKEY BURGERS WITH APPLE,
CARAMELIZED ONION & GOAT CHEESE

149 PARMESAN-CRUSTED CHICKEN
TENDERS WITH BUTTERMILK
RANCH DRESSING

151 CHICKEN SOUVLAKI WITH
TZATZIKI & FETA

157 BACON-WRAPPED PORK
TENDERLOIN WITH
GINGER APPLE COMPOTE

160 CASHEW & BASIL CHICKEN
LETTUCE WRAPS

163 SPICE-RUBBED STEAK WITH
GRILLED PEACHES & BLUE CHEESE

JERK SHRIMP SALAD WITH MANGO & AVOCADO

This tropical salad is a vacation, a retreat from the grilled chicken and mixed greens of our normal weekdays. The spicy jerk-seasoned shrimp can also make a great appetizer all on their own, with a bowl of the vinaigrette served on the side as a dipping sauce! But I adore the spices mixed with the fresh mango, avocado, and vegetables in this salad.

_____

1 In a large bowl, whisk together the brown sugar, garlic powder, oregano, thyme, allspice, nutmeg, cinnamon, salt, and cayenne. Add the shrimp and toss to coat well.

2 In a 12-inch nonstick skillet set over medium-high heat, heat 1 tablespoon of the oil. Add the shrimp and cook, undisturbed, until browned on one side, 2 to 3 minutes. Flip and cook until browned on the other side and opaque throughout, about 2 more minutes. Transfer to a plate.

3 In a large bowl, whisk together the lime juice, apricot preserves, and the remaining 2 tablespoons of olive oil. Add the romaine, cilantro, carrots, and mango, and toss to coat.

4 Divide the salad among 4 plates and top each with a quarter of the avocado and the shrimp.

Serves 4

PER SERVING	
Calories	394
Protein	30 g
Carbohydrates	26 g
Fiber	6 g
Sugar	19 g
Total Fat	20 g
Saturated Fat	3 g
Sodium	605 mg

2 teaspoons packed light brown sugar

1 teaspoon garlic powder

1 teaspoon dried oregano

1 teaspoon dried thyme

1/4 teaspoon allspice

1/4 teaspoon ground nutmeg

Pinch of ground cinnamon

1/2 teaspoon salt

1/4 teaspoon cayenne pepper

1 1/2 pounds large shrimp, peeled and deveined

3 tablespoons extra-virgin olive oil

2 tablespoons fresh lime juice

2 tablespoons all-fruit apricot preserves

1 large head romaine, chopped

2/3 cup chopped fresh cilantro

2 large carrots, cut into matchsticks (about 2 cups)

1 large mango, peeled, pitted, and cut into thin strips

1 avocado, peeled, pitted, and cut into thin strips

LEMON-HERB FISH
WITH CRISPY OVEN FRIES

Fish and chips is so charmingly New England, and that's probably a large part of why I love it so much. I grew up eating heaping plates of battered-and-fried fish, often down on Cape Cod, with sides of coleslaw and crispy fries that I dipped in little paper cups of ketchup. This is my recharged version. It's a whole lot lighter, with no deep frying involved, and the flavors are brighter, too, thanks to the perkiness of lemon and parsley. If you love a good crispy french fry, you'll be so impressed with this baked version. The secret? Soaking the potatoes in a hot water bath before baking. For a nice dinner, try serving this with Perfect Roasted Broccoli (page 100) for a little bit of green.

_1_   For the oven fries, preheat the oven to 450°F.

_2_   Put the potato sticks in a large bowl, fill with enough hot tap water just to cover them, and let stand for 10 minutes.

_3_   Drain the potatoes, spread them out on a large kitchen towel, and dry them well. Put the potatoes in a large bowl, add the oil, toss well, and spread them out on a wire rack set inside a large rimmed baking sheet. Season with the salt. Bake until golden brown and crispy, about 40 minutes.

_4_   About 20 minutes before the fries are done, prepare the fish. In the bowl of a food processor, combine the panko, garlic, parsley, lemon zest, salt, and pepper. Pulse until you have fine crumbs. Pour into a wide, shallow bowl.

_5_   In a separate shallow bowl, lightly beat the eggs. Dip both sides of 1 piece of fish first in the egg mixture, letting any excess drip off, and then dredge in the bread crumb mix, pressing to coat. Transfer the fish to a plate and repeat the process with the remaining 3 pieces of fish.

Serves 4

PER SERVING	
Calories	427
Protein	40 g
Carbohydrates	39 g
Fiber	3 g
Sugar	1 g
Total Fat	12 g
Saturated Fat	4 g
Sodium	774 mg

Oven Fries

1½ pounds (about 2 large) russet
    potatoes, cut lengthwise into
    ½-inch-thick sticks
1 tablespoon olive oil
½ teaspoon salt

Fish

¾ cup panko bread crumbs
3 garlic cloves
¼ cup packed fresh flat-leaf
    parsley
Zest of 1 lemon (about
    1 tablespoon)
½ teaspoon salt
½ teaspoon freshly ground
    black pepper
2 large eggs
1½ pounds cod or haddock
    filets, cut into 4 equal pieces
1 tablespoon unsalted butter

6   In a 12-inch nonstick skillet set over medium-high heat, heat
    ½ tablespoon of the butter. Add 2 of the pieces of fish and
    cook, undisturbed, until their undersides are crisp and lightly
    golden, 3 to 4 minutes. Flip and cook until the second side is
    crisp and lightly golden, 3 minutes more. Transfer to a warm
    plate. Add the remaining ½ tablespoon of butter, and repeat
    the cooking process with the remaining 2 pieces of fish.

7   Divide the fish and chips among 4 plates and serve
    immediately.

BROWN SUGAR & CHILI-RUBBED SALMON WITH AVOCADO CREMA

Do you ever make a meal and just know—I mean know, with absolute certainty—that somewhere in the Hamptons, Ina Garten would be, like, super proud of you? That even if she were completely absorbed in splitting vanilla beans for homemade extract, she would totally side-eye your dish and smile?

This is that meal. It's got caramelized lime slices, for heaven's sake! Ina would be positively smitten. What I love about it, and what I think you (and Ina) will, too, is that the brown sugar–chili rub gives the salmon a spicy-sweet quality, and a smokiness when it's nearly blackened in a hot pan. The crema—a silky blend of avocado, sour cream, lime juice, parsley, and garlic—is a nice, cooling balance. I love serving this flavorful fish with Mashed Sweet Potatoes with Orange Zest & Basil (page 95), and if I'm having guests for dinner, I'll even add the Arugula with Orange Segments, Spiced Walnuts & Goat Cheese salad (page 84).

---

1 For the avocado crema, in a blender or food processor, combine the avocado, sour cream, lime juice, garlic, parsley, and salt, and pulse until smooth. The consistency should be similar to sour cream—thick yet spreadable. To thin it, add a tablespoon or two of water and pulse to incorporate. Cover and set aside until ready to serve. The crema will keep in an airtight container in the refrigerator for 1 day.

2 For the salmon, in a small bowl, combine the sugar, chili powder, salt, and cayenne pepper. Lay the salmon filets on a clean work surface and sprinkle the brown sugar mixture evenly over each filet, rubbing it into the flesh on all sides.

3 In a 12-inch nonstick skillet set over medium-high heat, heat 2 teaspoons of the oil. Add 2 of the salmon filets (skin side up, if they have skin on) and cook, undisturbed, until their

recipe continues

Serves 4

PER SERVING	
Calories	344
Protein	33 g
Carbohydrates	6 g
Fiber	2 g
Sugar	3 g
Total Fat	21 g
Saturated Fat	4 g
Sodium	391 mg

Avocado Crema

½ avocado, peeled and pitted

2 tablespoons sour cream

2 tablespoons fresh lime juice

1 garlic clove

¼ cup packed fresh flat-leaf
    parsley

Pinch of salt

Salmon

1 tablespoon packed light brown
    sugar

1 tablespoon chili powder

½ teaspoon salt

Pinch of cayenne pepper

4 5-ounce salmon filets

4 teaspoons extra-virgin
    olive oil

1 lime, thinly sliced into rounds

undersides are crisp and just beginning to blacken, about 4 minutes. Flip the filets and cook until the fish feels firm to the touch, 4 minutes more. Transfer to a warm plate. Add the remaining 2 teaspoons of oil to the pan and swirl to coat. Repeat the cooking process with the remaining 2 filets of salmon. Set the salmon aside.

4   Add the lime slices to the skillet and cook just until they begin to caramelize, about 30 seconds. Flip and cook for an additional 30 seconds.

5   To serve, divide the salmon filets among 4 plates and spoon 2 tablespoons of crema over each. Press a caramelized lime slice into the crema to garnish.

SPICY TOFU STIR-FRY WITH BOK CHOY

We all need a go-to stir-fry recipe in our repertoire. It's the one you pull out when you're exhausted and in need of a quick meal on weeknights, the one you turn to when you're trying to eat lighter after an indulgent weekend. In short, it's dependable.

I created this recipe after attending a pork festival a few years ago. I was in need of a meal with tons of veggies and something—*anything*—other than meat. The result was a way of hitting the reset button: very fresh, delicious, and restorative.

1 For the sauce, in a small bowl, whisk together the broth, soy sauce, sherry, chili garlic sauce, sugar, sesame oil, cornstarch, and garlic. Set aside.

2 For the stir-fry, cut the block of tofu in half horizontally to get 2 layers, then cut each layer into 12 small squares. Press the squares with paper towels to remove any liquid. In a medium bowl, toss the tofu with the cornstarch to coat well.

3 In a 12-inch nonstick skillet set over medium-high heat, heat 1 tablespoon of the canola oil until it's shimmering. Add the tofu in a single layer and cook until golden brown and crispy on all sides, 6 to 8 minutes. Transfer the tofu to a warm plate.

4 Wipe out the skillet. Heat 1 teaspoon of the canola oil over medium-high heat until very hot. Add the bell pepper and snow peas and cook until they begin to brown and soften, about 2 minutes. Transfer to the plate with the tofu.

recipe continues

Serves 4

PER SERVING	
Calories	369
Protein	17 g
Carbohydrates	40 g
Fiber	6 g
Sugar	6 g
Total Fat	16 g
Saturated Fat	2 g
Sodium	691 mg

Sauce

¼ cup low-sodium chicken broth

2 tablespoons low-sodium soy sauce

2 tablespoons dry sherry

1 tablespoon Asian chili garlic sauce (I like Sambal Oelek)

1 tablespoon sugar

2 teaspoons toasted sesame oil

1 tablespoon cornstarch

1 garlic clove, minced

5 Add the remaining 2 teaspoons of the canola oil, bok choy, garlic, and ginger, and cook, stirring frequently, until the mixture begins to brown and soften, about 2 minutes.

6 Return the bell pepper, snow peas, and tofu to the skillet. Add the sauce and cook, stirring constantly, until the sauce has thickened, 2 to 3 minutes.

7 To serve, mound ½ cup rice on each of 4 plates and divide the stir-fry among the plates.

Stir-Fry

1 14-ounce block extra-firm tofu, dried with paper towels

2 tablespoons cornstarch

2 tablespoons canola oil

1 large red bell pepper, seeded, ribs removed, and sliced (about 1¼ cups)

4 ounces snow peas (about 2 cups)

1 pound bok choy, sliced on the bias into ¾-inch pieces (about 3 cups)

2 garlic cloves, minced

1 tablespoon finely chopped fresh ginger

2 cups cooked brown rice, for serving

HALIBUT BAKED IN PARCHMENT
WITH PISTACHIO MINT PESTO

Baking in parchment is one of the easiest, most convenient, and least fussy modes of meal prep around. But it's not just the ease I love; it's that this method creates a steaming effect that makes for flaky, tender fish every time. These halibut filets take a quick 15 minutes in the oven and emerge buttery and soft, with perfectly cooked veggies. I love the way pistachio mint pesto dresses up the fish and adds exciting flavor, but you could just as easily skip it if you're short on time.

Serves 4

PER SERVING	
Calories	395
Protein	42 g
Carbohydrates	12 g
Fiber	3 g
Sugar	5 g
Total Fat	19 g
Saturated Fat	5 g
Sodium	599 mg

1 For the pesto, in a food processor, pulse the parsley, mint, oil, pistachios, garlic, and salt until smooth, scraping down the sides of the bowl as needed. Scrape into a bowl and stir in the Parmesan cheese.

2 Preheat the oven to 450°F.

3 Cut eight 12-inch squares of parchment paper and lay 4 of them on a clean work surface. Divide the shallots, zucchini, squash, and carrots among the centers of the parchment sheets. Pour 1 tablespoon of the wine over each mound of vegetables. Season the halibut evenly with the salt and pepper, and place one filet on top of each vegetable mound. Top each filet with 1 teaspoon butter, 2 teaspoons lemon zest, and 1 slice of lemon. Place a second square of parchment on top of the halibut and fold the edges in a few times on all sides, sealing the edges by folding them over on themselves, creating a packet roughly 7 to 8 inches long. Place the packets on a large rimmed baking sheet.

Pesto

¼ cup packed fresh flat-leaf parsley

¼ cup fresh mint leaves

2 tablespoons extra-virgin olive oil

3 tablespoons shelled unsalted pistachios

2 garlic cloves

¼ teaspoon salt

2 tablespoons grated Parmesan cheese

4   Bake until the fish is cooked through and the vegetables are tender, about 15 minutes.

5   Serve the halibut and vegetables in the packets, taking care when opening the packets so the steam does not burn you. Drizzle the pesto evenly over the halibut filets after opening the packets.

Halibut

1 medium shallot, thinly sliced (about ¼ cup)

1 large zucchini, cut into matchsticks (about 2 cups)

1 large summer squash, cut into matchsticks (about 2 cups)

2 medium carrots, cut into matchsticks (about 2 cups)

¼ cup dry white wine or low-sodium chicken broth

4 6-ounce halibut filets

½ teaspoon salt

¼ teaspoon freshly ground black pepper

4 teaspoons unsalted butter

3 tablespoons grated lemon zest

1 lemon, thinly sliced

CREAMY FARRO WITH WHITE BEANS & KALE

My friend Sabrina's mom, Toni, loves to send me new ingredients to try in recipes, and farro was one of the first. For a month, this new-to-me grain sat in my cabinet, unused and unsure of itself, next to the quinoa and the brown rice. And then, one night, I plucked it out and made this recipe—one that I've made a dozen or so times since. Farro has a pleasing chewiness that you don't always get with other grains—perhaps with the exception of wheat berries. It's hearty; it sticks to your ribs. Here, I've added sautéed mushrooms, kale, and white beans, and just enough Gruyère and Parmesan cheeses to make a hint of a creamy sauce.

Serves 4

PER SERVING	
Calories	343
Protein	20 g
Carbohydrates	46 g
Fiber	11 g
Sugar	4 g
Total Fat	12 g
Saturated Fat	4 g
Sodium	708 mg

1 cup dry farro

3 cups low-sodium vegetable or chicken broth

1 bay leaf

1 15-ounce can white beans, rinsed and drained

2 ounces Gruyère cheese, shredded (about ½ cup)

3 tablespoons grated Parmesan cheese

4 teaspoons extra-virgin olive oil

8 ounces portobello mushroom caps, stems and gills removed, sliced into ½-inch pieces

1 medium shallot, thinly sliced (about ¼ cup)

3 garlic cloves, minced

1 small bunch kale, leaves chopped (about 4 cups chopped)

½ teaspoon salt

½ teaspoon freshly ground black pepper

2 tablespoons finely chopped fresh flat-leaf parsley

1 In a medium saucepan set over medium-high heat, bring the farro, broth, and bay leaf to a boil. Reduce the heat to medium-low and simmer until the grains are tender but still chewy, about 30 minutes.

2 Stir the beans into the hot grains. Add the Gruyère and Parmesan cheeses and stir until melted. Cover to keep warm.

3 Meanwhile, in a 12-inch nonstick skillet, heat 2 teaspoons of the oil over medium-high heat until very hot. Add the mushrooms and cook until browned on one side, 3 to 4 minutes, then stir and cook until browned and tender on the other side, 3 to 4 minutes more. Transfer the mushrooms to a warm plate.

4 Add the remaining 2 teaspoons of oil to the skillet along with the shallots and garlic and cook, stirring constantly, until the garlic is fragrant, about 30 seconds. Add the kale and cook, stirring frequently, until wilted, about 3 minutes. Season with the salt and pepper.

5 Stir the kale, mushrooms, and parsley into the farro and beans and serve immediately.

LIGHTENED-UP PAD THAI IN UNDER 15 MINUTES

When I was growing up in Medfield, Massachusetts, there were very few restaurant options if you weren't in the mood for pizza. Thai World, which has since closed its doors, was a blessing to our small town. The first time my mom and I ate there, I ordered the Chicken Pad Thai—which was surely the most exotic meal I'd ever eaten. A craving was born. This rendition of pad thai isn't authentic in two main ways: first, I chose not to use tamarind—an ingredient in most traditional recipes—because it can be hard to find and a bit of a hassle to prepare; second, I swapped out the rice noodles for shredded cabbage, cutting the carbs significantly. But the flavor, however inauthentic, is great.

Serves 2

PER SERVING	
Calories	407
Protein	21 g
Carbohydrates	29 g
Fiber	7 g
Sugar	15 g
Total Fat	25 g
Saturated Fat	5 g
Sodium	2061 mg

1 tablespoon low-sodium soy sauce

2 tablespoons fish sauce

¼ cup low-sodium chicken broth

1 tablespoon sugar

1½ teaspoons cornstarch

4 large eggs

4 teaspoons canola oil

1 jalapeño pepper, ribs and seeds removed, finely chopped (about 2 tablespoons)

1 small onion, thinly sliced (about 1 cup)

1 small green bell pepper, seeded, ribs removed, and thinly sliced (about 1 cup)

4 garlic cloves, minced

5 cups finely shredded green cabbage (about half a medium head)

½ cup packed roughly chopped fresh cilantro or Thai basil

2 tablespoons finely chopped dry-roasted unsalted peanuts

1   In a small bowl, whisk together the soy sauce, fish sauce, broth, sugar, and cornstarch.

2   In another small bowl, beat the eggs.

3   In a 12-inch nonstick skillet, heat 2 teaspoons of the oil over medium-high heat. Add the jalapeño, onion, and pepper, and cook, stirring frequently, until tender but still crisp, about 5 minutes.

4   Add the garlic and cook, stirring constantly, until fragrant, about 30 seconds. Transfer the vegetables to a plate.

5   Add the remaining 2 teaspoons of oil to the skillet. Add the cabbage and cook, stirring frequently, until tender but still crisp, about 5 minutes. Add the eggs and cook, stirring constantly, until just set, about 2 minutes.

6   Add the soy sauce mixture, stir well, bring the mixture to a boil, and cook until the cabbage is coated in a thick, glossy sauce. Stir in the onions and peppers. Remove the pan from the heat and stir in the fresh cilantro. Sprinkle the peanuts over top and serve.

SOUTHWESTERN PULLED CHICKEN WITH CILANTRO LIME SLAW

Inspired by traditional pulled pork, this saucy shredded chicken is lighter in calories, but just as flavorful. Using chicken thighs is key for super-tender meat—that and cooking it low and slow until it falls off the bone. My recipe has a bit of a kick to it, which is why I love serving it with a pile of cool, crisp slaw.

   If you should find yourself needing an extra crunch on the side—something like a potato chip—try the Kale Chips on (page 83). They'll hit that salty, crunchy spot!

1   Put the chicken in a 6-quart slow cooker. Scatter the onion over the chicken.

2   In a small bowl, combine the tomato sauce, vinegar, liquid smoke, garlic, brown sugar, coriander, cumin, chili powder, and chipotle chili, and stir well. Pour the mixture over the chicken.

3   Cook on low until the chicken thighs are pierced easily with a fork, about 8 hours. Using two forks, shred the chicken.

4   To serve, put the bottom halves of the sandwich buns on 6 plates. Divide the shredded chicken among the buns, arrange the avocado slices over the chicken, and top with the other halves of the buns. Serve with ½ cup cilantro lime slaw alongside each sandwich.

Serves 6

PER SERVING

Calories	452
Protein	34 g
Carbohydrates	38 g
Fiber	7 g
Sugar	8 g
Total Fat	19 g
Saturated Fat	3g
Sodium	349mg

2 pounds boneless skinless chicken thighs

1 large onion, chopped (about 1¼ cups)

1 14½-ounce can tomato sauce

2 tablespoons apple cider vinegar

1 teaspoon liquid hickory smoke

3 garlic cloves, minced

3 tablespoons packed light brown sugar

2 teaspoons ground coriander

2 teaspoons ground cumin

1 tablespoon chili powder

1 chipotle pepper in adobo sauce (from a can), chopped

6 whole-grain sandwich buns, sliced in half

1½ avocados, peeled, pitted, and thinly sliced

Cilantro Lime Slaw (recipe follows)

PER SERVING	
Calories	67
Protein	1 g
Carbohydrates	6 g
Fiber	2 g
Sugar	4 g
Total Fat	5 g
Saturated Fat	1 g
Sodium	61 mg

Cilantro Lime Slaw

Makes about 3 cups; serves 6

2 tablespoons extra-virgin olive oil

2 tablespoons fresh lime juice

2 teaspoons honey

1 teaspoon chili powder

⅛ teaspoon salt

3 cups finely shredded green cabbage (about a quarter of a large head or ½ pound)

1 large carrot, peeled and grated (about 1 cup)

¼ cup packed finely chopped fresh cilantro

In a large bowl, whisk together the oil, lime juice, honey, chili powder, and salt. Add the cabbage, carrot, and cilantro, and toss well. Cover and refrigerate until ready to serve, at least 30 minutes and up to 1 day. Note that the cabbage will soften and wilt the longer it sits.

"CAN YOU STAY FOR DINNER?"

* 🌼 *

I wish the four of us had more dinners together. Looking back, there were so few. And yet I remember the places where we sat around that butcher block table, the funny stories we told, the way we rested our elbows on the table, relaxing into one another's company. Mom would have made one of her specialties: meatloaf with mashed potatoes or baked haddock. Dad would be making us all laugh until we cried with wild stories from growing up. Anthony's stutter would all but disappear. For a time, we muted the world around us, forgetting that Mom would have to leave for her second shift in an hour, pretending that Dad wasn't an alcoholic.

When Dad died, it was as if dinners went with him. Mom worked even more, and with Anthony away at college, I was home alone eating cereal most nights. What saved me in those lonely years were my best friends, Kate and Nicole. Nearly every day after school, I'd go to one of their houses, and come six p.m., Kate's mom or Nicole's dad would look at me and ask, "Can you stay for dinner?" Even though they never said it, they knew I had no one to eat with at home. They knew I could stay, and I loved them for offering. I'd park myself at their tables, in time gaining my own spot at each house, and for at least the duration of the meal, I was part of a family.

I crave that family feel even now, in my hint of an apartment in Manhattan. No matter what chaos ensued during my day, no matter how tempted I might be to spoon peanut butter straight from the jar standing up, I make dinner every night— for myself and my best friend, Sabrina. On weekends, I'll invite friends over and I'll make something extra delicious. Sometimes we'll have sleepovers, even though we're thirty and can't keep our eyes open past midnight.

When I think of dinners growing up—in my own kitchen and the ones that welcomed me—I'm reminded of some of my favorite memories. I remember Dad at his best, Mom laughing as though she didn't have a care in the world, glasses clanking, talking with our mouths full, hands gesturing like charades—and whatever we ate becomes the least memorable part. It wasn't the food itself that gave dinner meaning—not then, not all these years later. Any contentment, any fullness I felt, never came on a plate, in a bowl—it never seemed to double when I ate more—because true happiness and joy were all right there, sitting beside and across from me at the table.

CHICKEN CURRY
WITH GINGER & YOGURT

Curries really pack a flavor punch, but they can often be overloaded with calories. To keep things light, I decided to use yogurt to add creaminess to this recipe instead of something like coconut milk, which is very high in fat and calories. It works beautifully! If you like, you can also serve this curry with basmati rice or naan bread.

1 For the marinade, in a small bowl, combine the yogurt, garlic, ginger, cumin, coriander, cayenne, and salt. Put the chicken in a gallon-size resealable plastic bag, add the marinade, seal the bag, and gently shake to coat the chicken well. Refrigerate for at least 2 hours and up to 24 hours.

2 For the curry, remove the chicken thighs from the marinade, discard the remainder of the marinade, and pat each thigh dry with paper towels.

3 In a 12-inch nonstick skillet set over medium-high heat, heat 2 teaspoons of the oil. Add the chicken thighs and cook, undisturbed, until browned on one side, 4 to 6 minutes. Flip the thighs and cook until cooked through, 4 to 5 more minutes. Transfer the thighs to a plate and tent with aluminum foil to keep warm.

4 In the same skillet set over medium heat, heat the remaining 2 teaspoons of the oil. Add the onion and cook, stirring frequently, until lightly golden and beginning to soften, about 4 minutes.

recipe continues

Serves 4

PER SERVING	
Calories	319
Protein	37 g
Carbohydrates	12 g
Fiber	2 g
Sugar	3 g
Total Fat	13 g
Saturated Fat	3 g
Sodium	514 mg

Marinade

½ cup plain whole-milk yogurt

3 garlic cloves, minced

2 tablespoons finely chopped fresh ginger

1 teaspoon ground cumin

1 teaspoon ground coriander

⅛ teaspoon cayenne pepper

½ teaspoon salt

1½ pounds boneless skinless chicken thighs

5 Add the garlic, ginger, jalapeño, cumin, curry powder, and coriander, and cook, stirring constantly, until it becomes a thick, fragrant paste, about 2 minutes.

6 Add the tomato sauce and salt and cook until the mixture comes to a simmer. Stir in the yogurt and cilantro and cook, stirring frequently, until the yogurt is warm, about 3 minutes.

7 Return the chicken thighs to the pan, turn them to coat them in the sauce, and cook until hot, 5 minutes. Serve hot.

Curry

4 teaspoons extra-virgin olive oil

½ cup finely chopped white onion

3 garlic cloves, minced

1 tablespoon finely chopped fresh ginger

1 jalapeño pepper, ribs and seeds removed, finely chopped (about 2 tablespoons)

1 teaspoon ground cumin

1 teaspoon ground coriander

2 teaspoons curry powder

1 15-ounce can tomato sauce

½ teaspoon salt

½ cup whole-milk yogurt

¼ cup packed finely chopped fresh cilantro

BEEF PUTTANESCA
WITH GARLIC BREAD

I've always loved the salty, briny flavor of authentic spaghetti alla puttanesca. And while spaghetti is nice, the sauce is really what I'm after. To spin the sauce into a heartier, more satisfying main course, I add beef and white beans, but feel free to omit one or both if you'd like; the sauce is plenty rich on its own. Do yourself a favor and ditch the spaghetti, as I do, then serve a quick-and-easy garlic bread on the side for dipping.

_____

1 For the beef, in a 12-inch nonstick skillet set over medium-high heat, sauté the ground beef, breaking it up with a rubber spatula, until browned, 6 to 8 minutes. Using a slotted spoon, transfer the beef to a plate and tent with foil to keep warm.

2 Using the same skillet, add the onion to the beef drippings and cook, stirring frequently, until the onion is just beginning to soften, 2 to 3 minutes. Add the garlic and cook, stirring constantly, until fragrant, 30 seconds.

3 Add the diced tomatoes and their juices and bring the mixture to a simmer. Add the beans and simmer for 3 minutes.

4 Add the artichokes, olives, and capers, and return the beef to the pan. Stir in the basil. Reduce the heat to low while you prepare the garlic bread.

5 For the garlic bread, preheat the oven to 400°F.

6 Slice the baguette in half lengthwise, and then in half widthwise, to create four 6-inch sections. Place the baguette pieces on a baking sheet cut sides up.

recipe continues

Serves 4

PER SERVING	
Calories	566
Protein	38 g
Carbohydrates	52 g
Fiber	8 g
Sugar	5 g
Total Fat	24 g
Saturated Fat	6 g
Sodium	1268 mg

Beef

1 pound ground sirloin (90% lean)

½ medium yellow onion, thinly sliced (about ½ cup)

3 garlic cloves, minced

1 15-ounce can diced tomatoes

1 15-ounce can cannellini beans, rinsed and drained

4 canned artichoke hearts (in water or brine), quartered

⅓ cup chopped pitted kalamata olives

2 tablespoons capers, rinsed and drained

½ cup packed chopped fresh basil leaves, plus more for serving

¼ cup grated Parmesan cheese, for serving

7 In a small nonstick skillet or saucepan, heat the olive oil over medium heat. Add the garlic and stir constantly until just faintly golden and fragrant, 1 to 2 minutes, lowering the heat if necessary so the garlic does not burn. Immediately remove the pan from the heat and pour the garlic oil into a small bowl.

8 In a small bowl, combine the oregano, red pepper flakes, and salt.

9 Using a pastry brush, brush each piece of baguette with the garlic oil. Sprinkle liberally with the oregano-pepper-salt mixture.

10 Bake until golden brown, 7 to 10 minutes

11 To serve, divide the puttanesca among 4 bowls. Garnish each bowl with 1 tablespoon of Parmesan cheese and more fresh basil, if desired. Serve with the garlic bread.

Garlic Bread

½ of a standard-size baguette
   or 1 demi-baguette
   (12 inches long)
2 tablespoons extra-virgin
   olive oil
3 garlic cloves, minced
1 tablespoon dried oregano
2 teaspoons crushed red
   pepper flakes
Pinch of salt

CHICKEN WITH SUN-DRIED TOMATOES & FETA

Something happens to me at the grocery store in my last five minutes of shopping: impulsivity. I'll get a flash of an idea and grab a few "last-minute items" that inevitably end up sitting in my cabinets for the rest of their lives. Jarred sun-dried tomatoes were one of those items until about a year ago, when I was sure I'd run out of ideas for chicken. For a dish that was born out of whim and poor planning, this recipe turned out to be an absolute gem. I chose to add feta for a tangy contrast to the sweet tomatoes, but goat cheese or fresh mozzarella work just as well.

The beauty of this meal is how quick it is, so I don't love the idea of making a time-intensive side to go along with it. Consider something simple, like whole-wheat couscous, which cooks up in no time, and a simple green salad.

---

1 Remove the sun-dried tomatoes from the jar, reserving 1 tablespoon of the oil. Press the tomatoes gently with paper towels to absorb most of the oil. Chop the tomatoes.

2 In a 12-inch nonstick skillet, heat the reserved tablespoon of oil from the jar over medium-high heat. Add the garlic and cook, stirring constantly, until fragrant, about 30 seconds. Add the chicken, season with the salt, pepper, and oregano, and cook until lightly browned on all sides, about 10 minutes. Add the sun-dried tomatoes and the feta, stir well, and cook until the feta is warm, about 2 minutes.

3 Divide the chicken among 4 plates, garnish with fresh basil, and serve immediately.

Serves 4

PER SERVING	
Calories	294
Protein	33 g
Carbohydrates	12 g
Fiber	3 g
Sugar	1 g
Total Fat	13 g
Saturated Fat	5 g
Sodium	648 mg

1 8-ounce jar sun-dried tomatoes packed in olive oil

4 garlic cloves, minced

1 pound boneless skinless chicken breasts, cut into thin strips

¼ teaspoon salt

¼ teaspoon freshly ground black pepper

1 tablespoon dried oregano

4 ounces feta cheese, crumbled (about 1 cup)

¼ cup chopped fresh basil leaves, for garnish

LEMON ROASTED CHICKEN WITH MOROCCAN COUSCOUS

I can't even list all the ways I use roasted chicken breasts. They're lifesavers, and cooking chicken with the skin on and the bone in makes for the most succulent, tender chicken around. For this particular dish, I've added lemon just to give it some freshness, and I created a quick pan sauce, but you can feel free to skip it. The Moroccan couscous—with its mixture of warm spices, pine nuts, and currants—adds enough flavor on its own.

For a delicious vegetable side, halfway through roasting the chicken, put a pan of Roasted Carrots with Honey Butter (page 92) in the oven alongside the chicken. You'll be so happy come dinnertime.

1 For the chicken, preheat the oven to 400°F.

2 Place the chicken breasts in a large baking dish. Carefully lift up the skin on each breast and season each evenly with 2 teaspoons of the garlic, 2 teaspoons of the lemon zest, and the parsley. Re-cover the breasts with the skin, rub the tops and sides evenly with the oil, and season with the salt and pepper.

3 In a small bowl, whisk together the chicken broth, the remaining 1 teaspoon of garlic, the remaining 1 teaspoon of lemon zest, and the lemon juice. Pour into the baking dish around the chicken.

4 Roast until the skin is crispy and golden and the chicken is cooked through, 35 to 40 minutes. Transfer the chicken to a cutting board and let rest for 5 minutes. Pour the juices from the baking dish into a small bowl and cover to keep warm.

recipe continues

Serves 4

PER SERVING	
Calories	410
Protein	36 g
Carbohydrates	24 g
Fiber	4 g
Sugar	1 g
Total Fat	18 g
Saturated Fat	5 g
Sodium	399 mg

Chicken

4 6-ounce bone-in, skin-on chicken breast halves

3 tablespoons minced garlic (about 4 large garlic cloves)

3 tablespoons grated lemon zest

3 tablespoons finely chopped fresh flat-leaf parsley, plus more for serving

1 tablespoon extra-virgin olive oil

½ teaspoon salt

¼ teaspoon freshly ground black pepper

⅓ cup low-sodium chicken broth

1 tablespoon fresh lemon juice

5   About 15 minutes before the chicken is done, begin preparing the couscous. In a small pot set over high heat, bring the chicken broth to a boil. Remove the pot from the heat and stir in the couscous, cumin, coriander, turmeric, lemon zest, salt, and pepper. Cover and let stand for 10 minutes. Fluff with a fork and stir in the butter, pine nuts, currants, and parsley.

6   To serve, divide the couscous among 4 plates and top each with a roasted chicken breast. Remove the chicken skin before eating and pour a tablespoon of the reserved pan juices over the top.

Couscous

1½ cups low-sodium chicken broth

¾ cup whole-wheat couscous

½ teaspoon ground cumin

½ teaspoon ground coriander

¼ teaspoon ground turmeric

2 teaspoons grated lemon zest

¼ teaspoon salt

¼ teaspoon freshly ground black pepper

1 tablespoon unsalted butter

¼ cup pine nuts

¼ cup currants (or golden raisins)

2 tablespoons finely chopped fresh flat-leaf parsley, plus more for serving

CHICKEN & MUSHROOMS IN MUSTARD MARSALA CREAM SAUCE

When I started my blog in 2010, this was the very first recipe I shared. It was Valentine's Day, and I had decided to throw a dinner party—which, thinking about it now, sounds like an odd time to throw a dinner party. Regardless, my guests came. They stayed. After appetizers and salad and wine, we feasted on this very dish. This recipe is a hands-down favorite of mine, and not just because it holds such a special place in my memory. It's one of the first dishes I lightened up, and it's still a go-to dish when I want something warm, rich, and comforting but that keeps my eating on track.

I serve this chicken alongside my Smashed Roasted Garlic Potatoes (page 89) for an even heartier, yet still balanced meal.

---

1 Spread the flour in a shallow baking dish. Pat the chicken dry with paper towels and season with the salt and pepper. Dredge one cutlet in the flour, coating both sides. Shake off the excess. Transfer to a plate and repeat with the remaining cutlets.

2 In a 12-inch nonstick skillet set over medium-high heat, heat 2 teaspoons of the oil. Add 4 of the cutlets to the pan and cook, undisturbed, until crisp and golden brown on the bottom, about 3 minutes. Flip the cutlets and cook for 2 more minutes. Transfer to a plate. Add another 2 teaspoons of the oil to the pan and repeat the cooking process with the remaining cutlets.

3 Place the remaining 2 teaspoons of the oil in the skillet, and add the onion and mushrooms. Cook, stirring occasionally, until browned and tender, about 4 minutes. Add the garlic and cook, stirring constantly, until fragrant, about 30 seconds.

recipe continues

Serves 4

PER SERVING	
Calories	402
Protein	44 g
Carbohydrates	15 g
Fiber	1 g
Sugar	6 g
Total Fat	14 g
Saturated Fat	5 g
Sodium	510 mg

¼ cup all-purpose flour

8 3-ounce thin chicken breast cutlets

½ teaspoon salt

½ teaspoon freshly ground black pepper

6 teaspoons extra-virgin olive oil

½ cup finely chopped yellow onion

8 ounces sliced mushrooms (about 2 cups)

3 garlic cloves, minced

½ cup dry Marsala wine

½ cup low-sodium chicken broth

2 ounces cream cheese, at room temperature

1 tablespoon Dijon mustard

¼ cup finely chopped fresh flat-leaf parsley

4   Add the wine and stir to scrape up any brown bits at the
    bottom of the pan. Add the broth and bring the liquid to a
    simmer. Cook until reduced by half and thickened, about
    7 minutes. Stir in the cream cheese and mustard until the
    cheese is melted and smooth.

5   Return the cutlets to the pan along with any juices that have
    accumulated on the plate and cook for 2 minutes. Stir in the
    parsley.

6   Divide the chicken and mushrooms among 4 plates and serve
    immediately.

SPAGHETTI WITH BRUSSELS SPROUTS & PANCETTA CREAM

This quick spaghetti dish reminds me of spaghetti carbonara—noodles coated in a creamy sauce studded with salty pancetta pieces. But carbonara isn't exactly a healthy dish—and the challenge with all pasta dishes is keeping them light and the portion sizes reasonable. So for this recipe, I cut down the amount of pasta and bulked up the dish with roasted Brussels sprouts. The simple pancetta cream sauce is made with full-fat, full-flavor ingredients, so I kept the amount low—just enough for a really delicious meal.

Serves 4

PER SERVING	
Calories	448
Protein	18 g
Carbohydrates	55 g
Fiber	10 g
Sugar	6 g
Total Fat	19 g
Saturated Fat	8 g
Sodium	957 mg

1   Preheat the oven to 425°F.

2   On a large rimmed baking sheet, toss the Brussels sprouts and olive oil. Spread in a single layer, cut sides down, and season with ¼ teaspoon of the salt. Roast until browned and tender, 30 to 35 minutes. Set aside.

3   In a 12-inch nonstick skillet set over medium-high heat, cook the pancetta until browned and crispy, 6 to 8 minutes. Transfer to a small bowl. Return the skillet to the stovetop.

4   Meanwhile, cook the pasta according to the package directions. Drain.

5   To the drippings in the pancetta skillet, add the leeks, the remaining ¼ teaspoon salt, and the pepper. Cook, stirring frequently, until the leeks begin to soften, 2 to 3 minutes. Add the garlic and cook, stirring constantly, until fragrant, about 30 seconds. Reduce the heat to low, add the half-and-half and chicken broth, and cook for 2 minutes. Add the spaghetti, pancetta, and Brussels sprouts, and toss to coat in the sauce. Stir in the Parmesan cheese.

6   Divide the pasta among 4 plates and serve immediately.

10 ounces Brussels sprouts, trimmed and quartered (about 4 cups)

2 teaspoons extra-virgin olive oil

½ teaspoon salt

4 ounces pancetta, finely chopped

8 ounces dry whole-wheat spaghetti

2 medium leeks, white and light-green parts only, thinly sliced (about 1½ cups)

¼ teaspoon freshly ground black pepper

3 garlic cloves, minced

½ cup half-and-half

¼ cup low-sodium chicken broth

¼ cup grated Parmesan cheese

TURKEY BURGERS WITH APPLE, CARAMELIZED ONION & GOAT CHEESE

If I were to list my favorite meals of all time, a good, juicy burger would easily be among the top three. Now, I know ground turkey doesn't quite excite your average burger lover in the same way that beef does. It's lean; it can dry out if you're not careful; it's mild in flavor. But my burgers are deliciously different. They stay moist because I add a little goat cheese and grated apple right into the patties. You'll love how well they pair with the sweet caramelized onions. What I serve these burgers with varies, but lots of times I'll eat them alongside my favorite Shredded Brussels Sprouts Salad (page 87). It's a foolproof meal for spring and summer get-togethers, too!

_____

1. For the caramelized onion, in a 12-inch nonstick skillet, heat the oil over medium heat. Add the onion and cook, stirring occasionally, until soft, about 10 minutes. Add the sugar and salt and cook, stirring occasionally, until the onion is a deep golden brown, about 12 more minutes. If the onion starts to burn, add a tablespoon of water to the pan. The onion will keep in an airtight container in the refrigerator for up to 5 days.

2. For the burgers, preheat the broiler. Line a broiler pan with aluminum foil and spray the foil with nonstick cooking spray.

3. In a small nonstick skillet, heat the oil over medium heat. Add the garlic and ginger and cook, stirring constantly, until fragrant, about 1 minute. Add the apple and cook, stirring frequently, until soft, about 3 minutes. Transfer the mixture to a small bowl and let cool slightly.

Makes 4 burgers; serves 4

PER SERVING	
Calories	430
Protein	37 g
Carbohydrates	32 g
Fiber	4 g
Sugar	10 g
Total Fat	17 g
Saturated Fat	7 g
Sodium	661 mg

Caramelized Onion

1 tablespoon extra-virgin olive oil

1 large yellow onion, thinly sliced (about 1¼ cups)

1 teaspoon sugar

Pinch of salt

Burgers

1 teaspoon extra-virgin olive oil

2 garlic cloves, minced

1 tablespoon finely chopped fresh ginger

½ large Granny Smith apple, peeled, cored, and finely grated (about ⅓ cup)

1 pound ground turkey breast

3 ounces goat cheese, crumbled (about ¾ cup)

2 scallions, white and
   light-green parts, finely
   chopped
1½ teaspoons dried thyme
½ teaspoon salt
½ teaspoon freshly ground
   black pepper

4 whole-grain sandwich buns,
   cut in half

4 In a large bowl, combine the ground turkey, goat cheese, scallions, thyme, salt, pepper, and the apple mixture. Mix well with your hands and form into 4 patties. Put the patties on the prepared pan. Broil 4 inches from the heat until the patties are cooked through, 5 to 6 minutes per side.

5 To serve, put the bottom halves of the sandwich buns on each of 4 plates. Put one patty on each of the bun halves, divide the caramelized onions evenly over the patties, and top with the other halves of the buns.

PARMESAN-CRUSTED CHICKEN TENDERS WITH BUTTERMILK RANCH DRESSING

You don't outgrow chicken tenders . . . it just doesn't happen. Some part of me will always be attached to the cute finger-size chicken pieces coated in crunchiness and always with something to dip them in. This version combines baking with a little bit of frying. I know it sounds like there's no way they'll compare, but trust me—these are wonderfully crunchy. My favorite dipping sauce is a homemade buttermilk ranch dressing, but you can of course substitute whatever you like!

Serves 4

PER SERVING	
Calories	312
Protein	33 g
Carbohydrates	7 g
Fiber	0 g
Sugar	1 g
Total Fat	16 g
Saturated Fat	4 g
Sodium	576 mg

½ cup panko bread crumbs

½ teaspoon garlic powder

½ teaspoon onion powder

¼ teaspoon salt

¼ teaspoon freshly ground
black pepper

¼ cup grated Parmesan cheese

4 egg whites

1 pound chicken breast
tenderloins

4 teaspoons extra-virgin
olive oil

Buttermilk Ranch Dressing
(recipe follows)

1 Preheat the oven to 400°F. Set a wire cooling rack over a large rimmed baking sheet. Spray the rack with nonstick cooking spray.

2 In a small shallow bowl, whisk together the bread crumbs, garlic powder, onion powder, salt, pepper, and Parmesan. In another small bowl, beat the egg whites.

3 Dredge each tender first in the egg whites, then in the bread crumbs, pressing to coat. Put the coated tenders on a plate as you go, repeating the dredging process until all the tenders are coated.

4 In a 12-inch nonstick skillet, heat 2 teaspoons of the oil over medium-high heat. Add half the tenders and cook until golden brown on one side, about 3 minutes. Flip and cook until the second side is golden brown, about 3 minutes more. Transfer to the prepared baking sheet. Add the remaining 2 teaspoons of oil to the pan, and repeat the cooking process with the remaining tenders.

5 Bake until the tenders are golden brown and cooked through, 8 to 10 minutes. Serve immediately with Buttermilk Ranch Dressing for dipping.

PER SERVING	
Calories	74
Protein	1 g
Carbohydrates	1 g
Fiber	0 g
Sugar	1 g
Total Fat	7 g
Saturated Fat	2 g
Sodium	205 mg

Buttermilk Ranch Dressing
Makes 1/2 cup; serves 4

2 tablespoons mayonnaise

2 tablespoons sour cream

1/4 cup low-fat buttermilk

1 tablespoon plus 1 teaspoon finely chopped fresh dill

1 1/2 teaspoons white wine vinegar

1/2 teaspoon garlic powder

1/4 teaspoon salt

1/4 teaspoon freshly ground black pepper

In a small bowl, whisk together the mayonnaise, sour cream, buttermilk, dill, vinegar, garlic powder, salt, and pepper. Cover and refrigerate until ready to use. Leftovers will keep covered in the refrigerator for up to 5 days.

CHICKEN SOUVLAKI
WITH TZATZIKI & FETA

I have a deep affection for street food. There's something about the right-nowness of the experience, the rush of being streetside, and the novelty of it all that just wins me over. And the cuisines—Greek, Mexican, Thai . . . the list is endless. Since a lot of street food isn't exactly light, I tried my hand at making souvlaki at home.

Serves 4

PER SERVING	
Calories	457
Protein	40 g
Carbohydrates	25 g
Fiber	0 g
Sugar	3 g
Total Fat	17 g
Saturated Fat	5 g
Sodium	619 mg

1 In a large bowl, whisk together the lemon juice, oil, garlic, parsley, oregano, and pepper. Add the chicken, toss to coat, cover the bowl, and refrigerate for at least 30 minutes and up to 8 hours.

2 Preheat a gas grill to high heat.

3 Thread the chicken onto presoaked wooden skewers (metal is OK, too), taking care to evenly distribute the pieces among the skewers. Grill, turning occasionally, until the chicken is browned on all sides and an instant-read thermometer registers 160°F, 18 to 20 minutes.

4 Arrange the pita breads directly on the grill grates and cook until warm and faintly charred, about 2 minutes per side.

5 Lay each warm pita bread on a plate and spread 1½ tablespoons of tzatziki on each. Divide the lettuce among the pita, arranging it in a line down the center of each, and repeat with the tomato, and feta. Slide the chicken off of the skewers and divide it among the pita. Wrap the sides of the pita inward over the chicken and vegetables and serve.

¼ cup fresh lemon juice (about 2 lemons)

3 tablespoons extra-virgin olive oil

2 garlic cloves, minced

2 tablespoons finely chopped fresh flat-leaf parsley

2 teaspoons dried oregano

½ teaspoon freshly ground black pepper

1¼ pounds boneless skinless chicken breasts, trimmed and cut into ¾-inch pieces

4 8-inch pita breads

Tzatziki Sauce (recipe follows)

2 cups chopped romaine lettuce

2 Roma tomatoes, chopped (about 2 cups)

2 ounces feta cheese, crumbled (about ½ cup)

PER 3 TBSP	
Calories	23
Protein	2 g
Carbohydrates	2 g
Fiber	0 g
Sugar	2 g
Total Fat	1 g
Saturated Fat	0 g
Sodium	161 mg

Tzatziki Sauce
Makes about 3/4 cup; serves 4

1 garlic clove, minced
¼ teaspoon salt
1 tablespoon fresh lemon juice
½ cup plain 2% Greek yogurt
¼ cucumber, peeled, halved lengthwise, seeded, and finely chopped
  (about ⅓ cup)
1 tablespoon finely chopped fresh mint leaves
1 tablespoon finely chopped fresh flat-leaf parsley

In a small bowl, combine the garlic and salt and, using the back of a spoon, mash the garlic into a paste. Stir in the lemon juice. Add the yogurt, cucumber, mint, and parsley, and stir well. The tzatziki will keep in an airtight container in the refrigerator for 4 days.

BACON-WRAPPED PORK TENDERLOIN WITH GINGER APPLE COMPOTE

A perfectly cooked pork tenderloin is something everyone should have in his or her repertoire. It's faithful, trustworthy. This one is first wrapped in bacon before it gets quickly seared on the stove and finished in the oven. Pork tenderloin is naturally lean, so the addition of bacon doesn't send this over the top health-wise. A sweet and gently spicy ginger apple compote is the companion pork needs—classic with a twist. I almost always round out this meal with Smashed Roasted Garlic Potatoes (page 89) or Arugula with Orange Segments, Spiced Walnuts & Goat Cheese (page 84). It's got a Sunday feel anytime.

Serves 4

PER SERVING	
Calories	339
Protein	37 g
Carbohydrates	16 g
Fiber	2 g
Sugar	14 g
Total Fat	13 g
Saturated Fat	4 g
Sodium	296 mg

1 1½-pound pork tenderloin
1 teaspoon garlic powder
¼ teaspoon salt
¼ teaspoon freshly ground black pepper
12 fresh sage leaves
4 slices bacon
2 teaspoons extra-virgin olive oil
Ginger Apple Compote (recipe follows)

1   Preheat the oven to 375°F.

2   Season the top and sides of the tenderloin with the garlic powder, salt, and pepper. Arrange the sage leaves over the top and along the sides, pressing them gently into the tenderloin so that they stick. Wrap the bacon slices evenly around the tenderloin, using kitchen twine to hold the bacon in place.

3   In a 12-inch nonstick skillet, heat the oil over medium-high heat. Add the tenderloin and cook, turning frequently, until the bacon is just crisp on all sides, about 8 minutes. Transfer to a roasting pan.

4   Roast until the bacon is crispy and browned and an instant-read thermometer inserted in the thickest part of the meat registers 140°F, 15 to 20 minutes. Transfer the pork to a cutting board and let it rest for 10 minutes before carving into ½-inch-thick slices.

5   Divide the slices among 4 plates and top with the compote.

PER ¼ CUP	
Calories	63
Protein	0 g
Carbohydrates	16 g
Fiber	2 g
Sugar	14 g
Total Fat	0 g
Saturated Fat	0 g
Sodium	2 mg

Ginger Apple Compote

Makes about 1 cup; serves 4

2 large sweet red apples (I like McIntosh or Cortland), peeled, cored, and
 finely chopped

2 tablespoons finely chopped fresh ginger

2 tablespoons packed light brown sugar

¾ teaspoon ground cinnamon

Pinch of ground nutmeg

1   In a small saucepan set over medium heat, combine the
    apples, ginger, sugar, cinnamon, and nutmeg with ¼ cup
    water. Bring to a simmer, stirring occasionally, and cook until
    the apples are tender, 10 to 12 minutes. Turn off the heat and
    let stand for 10 minutes to allow the juices to thicken.

2   The compote will keep in an airtight container in the
    refrigerator for 1 week.

CASHEW & BASIL CHICKEN LETTUCE WRAPS

One Saturday night about a year ago, I went out to eat at a local Chinese restaurant. Somehow, a week later, I found myself still thinking about—still craving—the incredible lettuce wraps I had. It wouldn't be quite so remarkable if it weren't for the facts that (a) we're talking lettuce, and (b) no part of lettuce is cake. I had to re-create them. These wraps manage to strike a delicate balance between sweet and salty, crunchy and tender, rich and refreshing.

Serves 4

PER SERVING	
Calories	371
Protein	17 g
Carbohydrates	40 g
Fiber	6 g
Sugar	6 g
Total Fat	16 g
Saturated Fat	2 g
Sodium	763 mg

½ cup unsalted cashews

¼ cup low-sodium chicken broth

3 tablespoons hoisin sauce

2 tablespoons low-sodium soy sauce

1 teaspoon sugar

1 teaspoon cornstarch

2 teaspoons canola oil

2 garlic cloves, minced

1 pound ground chicken breast

2 scallions, white and light-green parts, chopped

½ cup roughly chopped fresh basil leaves

1   Preheat the oven to 350°F. Spread the cashews on a baking sheet and toast until golden and fragrant, about 10 minutes. Let cool slightly, then chop the cashews and set aside.

2   In a small bowl, whisk together the broth, hoisin, soy sauce, sugar, and cornstarch.

3   In a 12-inch nonstick skillet set over medium-high heat, heat the oil. Add the garlic and cook, stirring constantly, until fragrant, about 30 seconds.

4   Add the chicken and cook, breaking up the meat with a spatula, until browned, 4 to 6 minutes.

5   Add the scallions and the hoisin sauce mixture and cook, stirring frequently, until the sauce thickens slightly, about 2 minutes. Stir in the basil and cashews.

6   To serve, divide the lettuce leaves among 4 plates and spoon the chicken mixture into each of the leaves.

SPICE-RUBBED STEAK WITH GRILLED PEACHES & BLUE CHEESE

I come from a real meat-and-potatoes lineage. It's the Irish in me. Steak was on my family dinner table at least once a week, and to this day, any special occasion is marked by a good cut of beef. Skirt steak—and flank, too—is one cut that takes well to rubs and marinades. This quick, salty spice rub tenderizes while adding big, bold flavor. If you haven't tried grilled peaches before, you've been missing out. I love the way they caramelize and pair with the savory beef and pungent blue cheese.

To make the meal even fresher tasting, I love to pair the steak with my Arugula with Orange Segments, Spiced Walnuts & Goat Cheese salad (page 84)—with or without the goat cheese, depending on how much cheese I'm in the mood for since there's blue cheese on the steak.

_____

1 In a bowl, combine the paprika, chili powder, garlic powder, cumin, oregano, brown sugar, cayenne, salt, and pepper. Pat the steak dry, then rub the spice mixture all over it. Cover and refrigerate for at least 1 hour and up to 24 hours.

2 Preheat a gas grill to medium-high heat.

3 Grill the steak with the lid covered, flipping halfway, until lightly charred, about 10 minutes for medium. Transfer the steak to a cutting board and let rest for 5 minutes before slicing it across the grain. Tent the steak loosely with foil to keep it warm while you make the peaches.

4 In a medium bowl, toss the peach slices with the oil. Grill the peach slices until lightly charred, about 4 minutes per side.

5 To serve, divide the sliced steak among 4 plates and top each with a quarter of the peach slices and a quarter of the blue cheese crumbles.

Serves 4

PER SERVING	
Calories	383
Protein	34 g
Carbohydrates	11 g
Fiber	2 g
Sugar	9 g
Total Fat	22 g
Saturated Fat	9 g
Sodium	681 mg

¼ teaspoon paprika

½ teaspoon chili powder

½ teaspoon garlic powder

½ teaspoon ground cumin

½ teaspoon dried oregano

2 teaspoons packed light brown sugar

⅛ teaspoon cayenne pepper

½ teaspoon salt

½ teaspoon freshly ground black pepper

1 1½-pound skirt steak

2 ripe peaches, pitted and cut into ½-inch-thick slices

2 teaspoons olive oil

3 ounces blue cheese, crumbled (about ¾ cup)

For Sharing

BAKED GNOCCHI WITH THREE CHEESES, *page 168*

BAKED GNOCCHI WITH
THREE CHEESES   **168**

MEATLOAF BURGERS WITH
BACON, PEPPER JACK &
FRIZZLED ONIONS   **169**

PJ'S MEATBALLS & SAUCE   **173**

SPICY CHIPOTLE CHICKEN
ENCHILADAS   **175**

WHITE PIZZA WITH
ROASTED GARLIC, RICOTTA &
EGGPLANT   **179**

CUBAN PULLED-PORK
SANDWICHES WITH
CARAMELIZED ONION &
THYME MAYO   **181**

CHEDDAR BISCUIT-TOPPED
BARBECUE CHICKEN PIE   **187**

LOADED CHORIZO NACHOS   **189**

BEEF STEW   **192**

LEMON CREAM RISOTTO   **195**

BAKED GNOCCHI
WITH THREE CHEESES

I first tasted gnocchi when I was in Florence, Italy. They were plump and soft, just as they should be. Like little potato marshmallows. I was enamored. Traditionally, gnocchi are served with a red sauce, or even pesto, but here I decided a rich sage-scented three-cheese treatment seemed like a nice departure. It's a classed-up version of baked macaroni and cheese. An ultimate comfort food, it's what I turn to for winter dinner parties when I know I have others coming to share the dish with me—and I can't be tempted to overdo it!

Serves 8

PER SERVING	
Calories	438
Protein	17 g
Carbohydrates	43 g
Fiber	2 g
Sugar	4 g
Total Fat	22 g
Saturated Fat	14 g
Sodium	893 mg

1 Preheat the oven to 375°F. Spray a 2-quart shallow baking dish with nonstick cooking spray.

2 In a large pot of boiling salted water, cook the gnocchi according to the package directions. Drain. Transfer to the prepared baking dish.

3 Meanwhile, in a medium saucepan set over medium heat, melt 4 tablespoons of the butter. While whisking constantly, add the flour and cook until you have a golden paste, about 3 minutes. Slowly whisk in the milk and the sage, bring the mixture to a simmer, and cook until thickened, 7 to 10 minutes. Add the Cheddar and 1 cup of the Parmesan and stir until melted. Stir in the Gorgonzola, salt, and pepper. Pour the sauce over the gnocchi and stir well.

4 In a small nonstick skillet set over medium-high heat, melt the remaining 2 tablespoons butter. Add the bread crumbs and cook, stirring, until golden, 3 minutes. Sprinkle the crumbs and the remaining 2 tablespoons Parmesan cheese over the gnocchi.

5 Bake until the sauce is bubbling and the topping is golden, 20 to 25 minutes.

2 16-ounce packages gnocchi

6 tablespoons (¾ stick) unsalted butter

4 tablespoons all-purpose flour

2 cups whole milk

6 fresh sage leaves, finely chopped

4 ounces sharp white Cheddar cheese, shredded (about 1 cup)

1 cup plus 2 tablespoons grated Parmesan cheese (about 4 ounces)

2 ounces Gorgonzola cheese, crumbled (about ½ cup)

½ teaspoon salt

½ teaspoon freshly ground black pepper

⅔ cup panko bread crumbs

MEATLOAF BURGERS
WITH BACON, PEPPER JACK
& FRIZZLED ONIONS

Back when I lived in the sweet little neighborhood of Queen Anne in Seattle, my boyfriend Daniel and I became regulars at the 5 Spot—the diner down the street. The inside was eclectic and weird—they played history tapes in the bathrooms—and they served big portions of hearty, stick-to-your-ribs comfort food. This meatloaf burger is a loving homage to their Longhorn Burger, which is what we always ordered. I changed it a little by starting with my favorite honey barbecue meatloaf recipe. And trust me, frying your own onion rings isn't as much of a challenge as it may seem. They're worth every second, every calorie—especially since they're an occasional treat.

1   In a large cast-iron skillet, cook the bacon over medium-high heat until crisp, 5 to 7 minutes. Transfer to a paper towel-lined plate. Drain the fat and wipe the pan with a paper towel.

2   In a large bowl, combine the ground beef, bread crumbs, Worcestershire sauce, mustard, barbecue sauce, honey, salt, and pepper. Using your hands, mix until just combined. Form the mixture into 4 patties.

3   In the same cast-iron skillet in which you cooked the bacon, heat the oil over medium-high heat until very hot. Add the burgers and cook until well browned and crisp crusted on one side, about 4 minutes. Flip the burgers and cook for 3 minutes more for medium doneness. Place the cheese on top of the burgers and continue cooking until melted, 1 to 2 minutes.

4   To serve, lay the bottom halves of the hamburger buns on a clean work surface. Put one patty on each of the bun halves. Break the bacon slices in half and place 2 halves on top of each patty, then top each with a quarter of the frizzled onions and the top half of the bun.

Serves 4

PER SERVING	
Calories	814
Protein	41 g
Carbohydrates	66 g
Fiber	3 g
Sugar	17 g
Total Fat	43 g
Saturated Fat	12 g
Sodium	1333 mg

4 slices bacon

1 pound ground sirloin
   (90% lean)

2/3 cup panko bread crumbs

1 tablespoon Worcestershire
   sauce

1 tablespoon Dijon mustard

1/4 cup smoky barbecue sauce

1 tablespoon honey

1/4 teaspoon salt

1/4 teaspoon freshly ground
   black pepper

1 tablespoon extra-virgin
   olive oil

4 ounces pepper Jack cheese
   (4 1-ounce slices or 1 cup
   shredded)

4 soft, fluffy white hamburger
   buns, split

Frizzled Onions (recipe follows)

PER ¾ CUP	
Calories	293
Protein	7 g
Carbohydrates	30 g
Fiber	2 g
Sugar	6 g
Total Fat	16 g
Saturated Fat	3 g
Sodium	376 mg

Frizzled Onions

Makes 3 cups

1 large egg

1 cup low-fat buttermilk

1 large yellow onion, very thinly sliced into rings (about 1¼ cups)

1 cup all-purpose flour

1 teaspoon garlic powder

½ teaspoon smoked paprika

½ teaspoon freshly ground black pepper

1 quart peanut oil, for frying

½ teaspoon salt

1   In a medium bowl, whisk together the eggs and buttermilk. Add the onion rings and toss to coat. Cover and refrigerate them for 30 minutes.

2   In a shallow baking dish or pie plate, whisk together the flour, garlic powder, paprika, and pepper.

3   In a heavy 2-quart saucepan, heat the oil over medium-high heat until it registers 375°F on a candy thermometer. Place the salt in a small bowl.

4   Using tongs, remove a handful of the onion rings from the buttermilk mixture, shake off the excess liquid, and toss them in the seasoned flour. Add the floured onion rings to the hot oil and fry until golden brown, 2 to 3 minutes.

5   Using a slotted spoon, remove the rings from the oil, place them on a paper towel–lined warm plate, and season with a generous pinch of the salt. Repeat with the remaining onions. Serve immediately.

PJ'S MEATBALLS & SAUCE

When my mom and my stepdad, Paul, fell in love—now over a decade ago—I began affectionately calling him "PJ," a shortening of Paul Joseph. It was meant to be a joke at first, but, well, somehow it stuck. Thankfully, he's kept it.

If you ask everyone who knows PJ what they love most about him, other than his being just about the kindest man around, most would answer that he has an incredible way with meatballs. He's famous for them. The sauce is sweeter and richer than most, and for our family it's a staple—simmered for hours before being served at holidays, parties, and (most important) times when I come home to visit. The ultra-tender meatballs are well seasoned with garlic and oregano, but it's the addition of mint that makes them so unique. I'll never be able to give them up, which means making them is always an excuse to invite friends over for dinner.

---

1 For the sauce, in a large pot, heat the oil over medium heat. Add the onion and cook, stirring occasionally, until it begins to brown, about 12 minutes. Lower the heat to medium-low and if the onion starts to burn, add a tablespoon of water.

2 Add the garlic and cook, stirring constantly, until golden and fragrant, about 1 minute. The more color that develops on the onion and garlic, the more flavor they'll add to the finished sauce.

3 Add the crushed tomatoes and tomato paste and stir well. Add the sugar, oregano, salt, and pepper. Bring the mixture to a simmer, reduce the heat to low, cover, and cook, stirring occasionally so that the bottom does not burn, for at least 30 minutes.

recipe continues

Serves 4

PER SERVING	
Calories	954
Protein	48 g
Carbohydrates	110 g
Fiber	12 g
Sugar	26 g
Total Fat	36 g
Saturated Fat	12 g
Sodium	1262 mg

Sauce

3 tablespoons olive oil

1 small onion, finely chopped (about ½ cup)

4 garlic cloves, minced

1 28-ounce can crushed or puréed tomatoes

1 6-ounce can tomato paste

2 tablespoons sugar

1 tablespoon dried oregano

¼ teaspoon salt

1 teaspoon freshly ground black pepper

4   Meanwhile, for the meatballs, break the beef apart into a large bowl. Add the egg, bread crumbs, oregano, mint, salt, and pepper. Using your hands, mix until well blended. Do not overwork the beef, or the meatballs will be tough.

5   Shape the mixture into about twelve 1½-inch balls. Drop them into the sauce and stir gently to cover the meatballs in sauce. Cover the pan and cook, stirring occasionally to prevent burning, until the meatballs are cooked through, about 1 hour.

6   Boil the pasta according to the package directions. Drain.

7   To serve, divide the pasta among 4 plates or bowls. Put 3 meatballs on top of each plate of pasta and pour ½ cup of the sauce over the meatballs and pasta. Sprinkle with the grated Parmesan cheese.

Meatballs

1 pound ground beef (preferably 85% lean)
1 large egg, lightly beaten
⅓ cup Italian-seasoned bread crumbs
2 teaspoons dried oregano
1½ teaspoons dried mint
½ teaspoon salt
½ teaspoon freshly ground black pepper

12 ounces dry penne or ziti
½ cup grated Parmesan cheese, for serving

SPICY CHIPOTLE CHICKEN ENCHILADAS

Enchiladas are such a popular meal, all across the country. I get it, they're hard to beat! Here I've taken the traditional chicken enchilada to an even richer level, if you can believe it, thanks to a rich chipotle cream and an ungodly amount of sharp Cheddar. This is a special-occasion meal, after all. If you haven't made your own enchilada sauce before, don't hesitate—it's quick, easy, and super flavorful. Feel free to kick up the heat with some cayenne or hot sauce.

1   For the enchilada sauce, in a medium saucepan set over medium-high heat, heat the olive oil. Add the onion and cook, stirring occasionally, until lightly browned and softened, about 6 minutes. Add the garlic and chipotle pepper, and cook, stirring constantly, until fragrant, about 30 seconds.

2   Add the tomato sauce, broth, chili powder, cumin, brown sugar, and salt, and bring to a boil. Reduce the heat to medium-low, and simmer for 10 minutes. Cover and keep warm until ready to use. The sauce can be made up to 2 days in advance and stored, covered, in the refrigerator until ready to use. Reheat in a small saucepan over medium heat on the stovetop.

3   For the chicken, preheat the oven to 425°F.

4   Pat the chicken dry with paper towels. Put it in a baking dish, rub with the oil, and season with the salt and pepper. Roast until the skin is browned and crispy and an instant-read thermometer inserted in the thickest part of the meat registers 160°F, 35 to 40 minutes. Let cool on a cutting board for 15 minutes. Remove the skin, pull the meat from the bone, and shred the meat.

recipe continues

Serves 6

PER SERVING	
Calories	636
Protein	44 g
Carbohydrates	41 g
Fiber	2 g
Sugar	4 g
Total Fat	34 g
Saturated Fat	13 g
Sodium	1135 mg

Enchilada Sauce

1 tablespoon extra-virgin olive oil

1 small yellow onion, finely chopped (about ½ cup)

2 garlic cloves, minced

1 chipotle pepper in adobo sauce (from a can), finely chopped

1 14.5-ounce can tomato sauce

1 8-ounce can tomato sauce

1 cup low-sodium chicken broth

2 tablespoons chili powder

1 tablespoon ground cumin

2 teaspoons packed light brown sugar

¼ teaspoon salt

5 Transfer the chicken to a large bowl, stir in ½ cup of the enchilada sauce, and let the chicken cool completely. Stir in the cilantro and pepper Jack cheese.

6 For the enchiladas, preheat the oven to 400°F. Spread 1 cup of the enchilada sauce evenly over the bottom of a 9 × 13-inch baking dish.

7 On a clean work surface, spread ⅓ cup of the chicken filling down the center of each tortilla. Roll each tortilla tightly and place in the baking dish, seam side down. Pour the remaining sauce evenly over the top of the enchiladas so that it covers each one. Sprinkle the Cheddar cheese over the top and cover the dish with aluminum foil.

8 Bake until warmed through and the cheese is melted, about 25 minutes. Serve immediately, 2 enchiladas per person. If desired, spoon 1 tablespoon of sour cream on top of each serving and sprinkle the scallions and cilantro over the top of all.

Chicken

1¾ pounds bone-in, skin-on chicken breast halves

2 teaspoons extra-virgin olive oil

¼ teaspoon salt

¼ teaspoon freshly ground black pepper

½ cup packed chopped fresh cilantro, plus more for serving

8 ounces pepper Jack cheese, shredded (about 2 cups)

Enchiladas

12 6-inch flour tortillas (I like La Tortilla Factory brand)

4 ounces sharp Cheddar cheese, shredded (about 1 cup)

⅓ cup sour cream, for serving

3 scallions, white and light-green parts, chopped, for serving

WHITE PIZZA WITH ROASTED GARLIC, RICOTTA & EGGPLANT

I've never met a pizza I didn't immediately take to, and that's somewhere between being a gift and a problem. Some of the most memorable ones have been the simplest. A classic margherita pie in Rome. The white pizza from Delancey in Seattle. There's something wonderful about the simple comfort of a good chewy crust and a few fantastic toppings—red sauce not necessarily required. This pie is wild with flavor. Roasted garlic—a truly transformative substance— is smeared all over the crust and then topped with crispy fried eggplant, thin slices of salty prosciutto, and dollops of creamy whole-milk ricotta. It's an indulgence, for sure!

———————

1   For the roasted garlic, preheat the oven to 400°F.

2   Peel as much of the loose, papery skin off the head of garlic as you can, leaving the bulb intact. Slice about ¼ inch off the top of the garlic so that you see the individual garlic cloves, then drizzle 1 teaspoon of the oil evenly over them.

3   Wrap the head in foil and bake until the cloves are golden and completely soft, about 45 minutes. Let cool for 10 minutes, then gently squeeze the bottom of the garlic head to pop the cloves out into a small bowl. Mash the cloves with the back of a spoon until smooth, add the remaining 1 tablespoon of the oil, and stir to combine into a silky paste.

4   For the eggplant, lay the slices on a wire rack set over a large rimmed baking sheet, then sprinkle them with the ½ teaspoon of salt to draw their extra moisture out. Let sit for 1 hour. Pat the slices dry with paper towels.

recipe continues

Serves 4

PER SERVING

Calories	800
Protein	32 g
Carbohydrates	83 g
Fiber	4 g
Sugar	10 g
Total Fat	37 g
Saturated Fat	9 g
Sodium	1893 mg

Roasted Garlic

1 head of garlic
1 tablespoon plus 1 teaspoon extra-virgin olive oil

Eggplant

½ medium eggplant, cut into ½-inch slices (6 to 8 slices)
½ teaspoon salt
½ cup all-purpose flour
2 large eggs, beaten
½ cup Italian-seasoned bread crumbs
4 tablespoons extra-virgin olive oil

5   Put the flour in a small shallow bowl, the beaten eggs in another small shallow bowl, and the bread crumbs in a third small shallow bowl. Dredge one eggplant slice first in the flour, then dip it into the eggs, and finally dip it into the bread crumbs, pressing to coat both sides. Transfer to a large plate and repeat with the remaining eggplant slices, taking care not to overlap them.

6   In a 12-inch nonstick skillet set over medium-high heat, heat 2 tablespoons of the oil. Add 4 of the eggplant slices and cook until browned and crispy on one side, 3 to 4 minutes. Flip and cook until browned on the other side, 2 to 3 more minutes. Transfer to a wire rack, add the remaining 2 tablespoons of the oil to the skillet, and repeat the cooking process with the remaining eggplant. Lower the heat, if necessary, to prevent burning.

7   For the pizza, preheat the oven to 500°F.

8   On a lightly floured work surface, stretch the dough into a 14-inch circle. Lay the dough on a large baking sheet. Spread the soft roasted garlic paste all over the dough, leaving a 1-inch border. Arrange the eggplant slices over the pie, drop dollops of the ricotta over the eggplant, then scatter the prosciutto over the top. Sprinkle with the Parmesan cheese.

9   Transfer the pie to the oven and bake until the crust is golden brown, 12 to 15 minutes. Cut into 8 slices, garnish with the basil, and serve.

Pizza

1 pound store-bought pizza dough

¾ cup whole-milk ricotta cheese

¼ pound thinly sliced prosciutto, torn or cut into thin strips

3 tablespoons grated Parmesan cheese

½ cup packed roughly chopped fresh basil leaves

CUBAN PULLED-PORK SANDWICHES WITH CARAMELIZED ONION & THYME MAYO

One of the best things I've ever eaten is the Caribbean Roast sandwich from Paseo in Seattle. I'd describe the place as a hole-in-the-wall, because that's what it is and what it looks like, but that wouldn't be fair. The spot is famous, and the sandwich is a Seattle legend: tender, slow-roasted pork shoulder with cilantro, roasted garlic aioli, and caramelized onions piled into a crusty baguette. Lines wrap around the block for it. Here is my loving tribute to that dynamo of a sandwich.

1 For the marinade, in a small bowl, combine the orange juice, rum, lime juice, minced garlic, and oregano. Cut 1-inch-deep slits all over the pork and place it in a gallon-size resealable plastic bag. Pour the marinade over the top, seal the bag, and shake it gently to coat the pork. Refrigerate overnight, for at least 8 hours and up to 24 hours.

2 Remove the pork from the bag and transfer it to the base of a standard 6-quart slow cooker. Pour ½ cup of the marinade in the base of the slow cooker and discard the rest.

3 In a food processor, pulse the orange juice, garlic, thyme, oregano, cumin, the ½ teaspoon of salt, pepper, and oil until smooth, about 3 pulses. Rub the paste all over the pork and into the slits. Cook on low until the pork is tender and no longer pink in the center, about 8 hours depending on the settings of your slow cooker. Using two forks, pull the pork into large chunks.

4 For the caramelized onion, in a 12-inch nonstick skillet set over medium heat, heat the oil. Add the onion and cook, stirring occasionally, until soft, 10 minutes. Add the sugar and

recipe continues

Serves 4

PER SERVING	
Calories	727
Protein	35 g
Carbohydrates	28 g
Fiber	2 g
Sugar	18 g
Total Fat	36 g
Saturated Fat	7 g
Sodium	637 mg

Marinade

2 cups orange juice

2 tablespoons dark rum

2 tablespoons fresh lime juice (1 lime)

3 garlic cloves, minced

2 tablespoons finely chopped fresh oregano leaves

Pork

1 2-pound pork shoulder

3 tablespoons orange juice

2 tablespoons finely chopped fresh thyme leaves

2 tablespoons finely chopped fresh oregano leaves

1 tablespoon ground cumin

½ teaspoon salt

½ teaspoon freshly ground black pepper

1 tablespoon extra-virgin olive oil

salt and cook, stirring occasionally, until the onion is a deep golden brown, about 12 minutes more. If the onion starts to burn, add a tablespoon of water to the pan. The caramelized onion will keep in an airtight container in the refrigerator for 5 days.

5   To assemble the sandwiches, lay the 8 baguette pieces on a clean work surface, cut sides up. Spread 2 tablespoons of the Thyme Mayonnaise on each of half of the baguette pieces. Divide the pork among half of the baguette pieces and top first with the lettuce, then with the onion, then with the fresh cilantro and the other halves of the baguettes. Serve.

Caramelized Onion

1 large yellow onion, thinly
   sliced (about 1¼ cups)
2 teaspoons sugar
Pinch of salt

1 large crusty baguette (about
   16 inches long), sliced in
   half lengthwise and cut into
   4 equal portions
2 cups finely chopped romaine
   lettuce, for serving
½ cup packed chopped fresh
   cilantro, for serving
Thyme Mayonnaise (recipe
   follows)

PER SERVING	
Calories	203
Protein	0 g
Carbohydrates	1 g
Fiber	0 g
Sugar	0 g
Total Fat	22 g
Saturated Fat	3 g
Sodium	151 mg

Thyme Mayonnaise
Makes ½ cup

2 garlic cloves, minced
Pinch of salt
1 tablespoon fresh lime juice (about ½ lime)
½ cup mayonnaise
2 teaspoons finely chopped fresh thyme

_____

In a small bowl, using a fork, mash the garlic with the salt and lime juice. Let stand for 5 minutes to allow the acidity of the lime to soften the garlic. Stir in the mayonnaise and thyme. The thyme mayonnaise will keep in an airtight container in the refrigerator for 3 days.

CELEBRATING AND ENJOYING

* ❋ *

When I moved to New York City two falls ago, I was convinced that the only way to mark my fresh start in a new city was by hosting a dinner party. Sabrina and I didn't even have a couch, and yet ten of our closest friends came over to enjoy a nice meal on the floor. I pored over recipes, unsure of how to strike the right tone. "Everyone likes Italian, right?" I asked Sabrina. The day of our party, we made a huge grocery run, gathering all the ingredients for butternut squash lasagna with browned butter–sage cream sauce, the necessities for PJ's meatballs, two loaves of ciabatta, more garlic and butter than we'd need in a year, the makings of blue cheese–stuffed dates wrapped in bacon, and so, so much more.

When we got home and I got to cooking, I realized we'd bought too much—easily enough food to feed twenty-five people—not just the ten coming. It was then that I knew I had become my mother. She's known up and down the Eastern Seaboard for setting the perfect table and serving at least triple the amount of food necessary for the number of people invited. Her style is chic-meets-Oprah-level generosity. She knows just how to make guests feel like they're always welcome. Unpacking the groceries, I thought, *She'd be so proud.*

I made the meal, sweating the whole way through in our tiny kitchen. Sabrina made us all cranberry ginger cocktails and hung the last of the pictures we'd been procrastinating putting up. The guests arrived, we chatted, we drank, ate hors d'oeuvres, and just past 7:30, we served dinner. As I made my plate—a square of lasagna, two meatballs, a mound of salad, and a small slice of garlic bread—I breathed a quiet sigh, remembering that just seven years earlier, I would have felt paralyzed by such a spread.

In the past—in the years when I was big—an abundant meal like this one would have sent me into an overeating frenzy that would have ended with me completely stuffed in a pants-undone, short-of-breath Thanksgiving way. And then I'd continue with a week-long binge. But after I started losing weight, I had an equally extreme but opposite reaction: I was terrified of food. I worried so much about not being able to control myself and eating too much that I withdrew.

In the end, after lots of hard work, I came to internalize the fact that I don't have to live in the extremes. That I don't have to pick either eating and being fat *or* starving and being skinny—that there's a place in between where I'm actually happiest. That place was mindfulness.

Sitting in my new New York City home, surrounded by dear friends and an overabundance of food, I reflected on the journey to that moment. I could enjoy decadent sandwiches, nachos piled high, and gooey mac and cheese; I just needed to be mindful of how much and how frequently I ate them. The key to enjoying these foods, and changing my relationship with them, was in making them special, in keeping them as once-in-a-while meals. And ones that I shared with people I love.

CHEDDAR BISCUIT-TOPPED BARBECUE CHICKEN PIE

Chicken pot pie is pure comfort food. It's a pie for dinner, for crying out loud. While traditional recipes call for pie dough on the top and bottom, my version gets a little bit southern with a flaky Cheddar biscuit crust covering barbecue-sauced chicken. I love pushing my fork through the buttery biscuit and into that smoky rich sauce, especially on a cold night. This is one of those meals you can make on Sunday—just in time for that marathon TV-watching party.

Serves 8

PER SERVING	
Calories	542
Protein	28 g
Carbohydrates	45 g
Fiber	4 g
Sugar	9 g
Total Fat	28 g
Saturated Fat	17 g
Sodium	710 mg

Chicken

2 pounds bone-in, skin-on chicken breasts

¼ teaspoon salt

¼ teaspoon freshly ground black pepper

Biscuit Topping

2 cups all-purpose flour

1 tablespoon baking powder

½ teaspoon baking soda

2 teaspoons sugar

1 teaspoon garlic powder

½ teaspoon salt

6 tablespoons (¾ stick) unsalted butter, cold and cut into pieces

1 tablespoon melted unsalted butter, for brushing the tops of the biscuits

1 cup buttermilk

1   For the chicken, preheat the oven to 400°F. Place the chicken breasts on a large baking sheet, rub them with the oil, salt, and pepper. Roast until the skin is crispy and the chicken is cooked through, 35 to 40 minutes. Let cool for 10 minutes. Remove the skin, pull the chicken off the bone, and chop the chicken. Increase the oven temperature to 450°F.

2   For the biscuit topping, in the bowl of a food processor, pulse the flour, baking powder, baking soda, sugar, garlic powder, and salt. Add the cold butter pieces and pulse until the mixture is crumbly and resembles cornmeal, about 7 pulses.

3   Transfer the mixture to a bowl and add the buttermilk. Using a rubber spatula, stir just until combined. Stir in the cheese and chives. The dough will be wet and lumpy.

4   Turn the dough onto a clean, lightly floured work surface and knead it 3 to 4 times, just until it comes together. Dust a rolling pin with flour and roll the dough into a 7 × 10-inch rectangle, about 1 inch thick. Using the rim of a drinking glass or a biscuit cutter, cut 8 rounds out of the dough. Place the biscuits on a parchment paper–lined plate and refrigerate while you make the filling.

recipe continues

5   For the filling, spray a 9 × 13-inch baking dish with nonstick cooking spray. Set aside.

6   In a large pot, melt the butter over medium-high heat. Add the onion, celery, carrots, salt, and pepper, and cook, stirring frequently, until soft, 6 to 8 minutes.

7   Add the mushrooms and cook, stirring occasionally, until soft, about 5 minutes. Add the garlic and cook, stirring constantly, until fragrant, 30 seconds. Add the peas and corn. Add the flour and cook, stirring constantly, until the vegetables are completely coated, 2 minutes.

8   Slowly add the broth and the heavy cream and bring the mixture to a gentle boil. Reduce the heat to medium-low and simmer, stirring frequently, until thickened, 4 to 6 minutes. Stir in the barbecue sauce and parsley.

9   Add the chicken, toss to coat, and transfer the mixture to the baking dish. Bake for 15 minutes. Remove the dish from the oven, top with the biscuits, and brush the tops of the biscuits with the melted butter. Bake until the biscuits are golden brown, 10 to 12 minutes.

4 ounces extra-sharp Cheddar cheese, shredded (about 1 cup)
1 tablespoon finely chopped fresh chives

Filling

2 teaspoons extra-virgin olive oil
½ teaspoon salt
¼ teaspoon freshly ground black pepper
5 tablespoons (½ stick plus 1 tablespoon) unsalted butter
1 medium onion, chopped (about 1 cup)
3 celery stalks, chopped (about 2 cups)
3 large carrots, chopped (about 2¼ cups)
1 cup button mushrooms, stems removed, chopped
3 garlic cloves, minced
1 cup frozen green peas, thawed
1 cup frozen corn kernels, thawed
⅓ cup all-purpose flour
2 cups low-sodium chicken broth
¼ cup heavy cream
¼ cup barbecue sauce (I like Sweet Baby Rae's)
2 tablespoons finely chopped fresh flat-leaf parsley, plus more for serving

LOADED CHORIZO NACHOS

Sitting around a towering, smothered pile of nachos with my best friends is one of life's pure pleasures. It's Friday nights and margaritas. It's overflowing laughter and telling each other everything. Chorizo adds such smoky, deep flavor to these nachos. Combined with spicy homemade queso, quick refried beans, and fresh pico de gallo, they're just about the most intense conversation starter around.

---

1   For the refried beans, in a food processor, pulse the broth and beans until smooth, but still slightly chunky, about 4 pulses.

2   In a small nonstick skillet, cook the bacon until crisp, about 5 minutes. Transfer to a paper towel–lined plate. Add the onion and cook, stirring frequently, until softened, about 4 minutes.

3   Add the garlic, cumin, coriander, chili powder, and cayenne, and cook, stirring constantly, until fragrant, about 30 seconds. Add the beans and stir until combined. Reduce the heat to medium and cook until the beans are thick and creamy, about 5 minutes. Finely crumble the bacon and stir it into the beans, along with the lime juice.

4   For the queso, in a medium saucepan, melt the butter over medium heat. Add the flour and cook, whisking constantly, until the mixture becomes a thick paste, about 30 seconds. Slowly whisk in the milk and cook, whisking frequently, until thickened, about 2 minutes. Stir in the Cheddar and American cheeses, green chiles, garlic powder, onion powder, and pepper, and cook until the cheeses have melted, about 1 minute.

recipe continues

Serves 8

PER SERVING	
Calories	855
Protein	33 g
Carbohydrates	48 g
Fiber	3 g
Sugar	6 g
Total Fat	61 g
Saturated Fat	25 g
Sodium	1421 mg

Refried Beans

¼ cup low-sodium chicken broth

1 15-ounce can pinto beans, rinsed and drained

3 slices bacon

¼ cup finely chopped red onion

2 garlic cloves, minced

½ teaspoon ground cumin

¼ teaspoon ground coriander

½ teaspoon chili powder

⅛ teaspoon cayenne pepper

1 teaspoon fresh lime juice

Queso

2 tablespoons unsalted butter

2 tablespoons all-purpose flour

1 cup whole milk

8 ounces Cheddar cheese, shredded (about 2 cups)

4 ounces white American cheese, chopped

1 4-ounce can green chiles

¼ teaspoon garlic powder

¼ teaspoon onion powder

¼ teaspoon freshly ground black pepper

5 For the chorizo, in a 12-inch nonstick skillet, heat the oil over medium-high heat. Add the onion and cook, stirring occasionally, until softened, about 4 minutes. Add the jalapeño, garlic, cumin, coriander, cayenne, and oregano, and cook, stirring constantly, until fragrant, about 1 minute. Add the chorizo and cook, breaking up the meat with a wooden spoon, until the chorizo is browned, 6 to 8 minutes. Transfer to a plate.

6 To assemble the nachos, on a large platter, spread a single layer of tortilla chips. Spoon half of the chorizo over the chips, followed by dollops of half of the refried beans and a drizzle of the queso. Repeat the layering once more. Garnish with the pico de gallo, scallions, cilantro, and, if desired, the shredded lettuce and sour cream. Serve immediately.

Chorizo

1 tablespoon olive oil
1 small yellow onion, finely chopped (about ½ cup)
1 jalapeño pepper, ribs and seeds removed, finely chopped (about 2 tablespoons)
2 garlic cloves, minced
½ teaspoon ground cumin
½ teaspoon ground coriander
¼ teaspoon cayenne pepper
¼ teaspoon dried oregano
1 pound Mexican-style chorizo, casings removed if necessary

Nachos

1 large bag restaurant-style tortilla chips
¾ cup store-bought pico de gallo
2 scallions, white and light-green parts, chopped, for serving
½ cup packed chopped fresh cilantro, for serving
1 cup shredded iceberg lettuce (optional)
½ cup sour cream (optional)

BEEF STEW

When I was sixteen, my mom fell in love with my stepdad, PJ.
Together they bought a house, and we all moved in together. Beyond
the joy of knowing that Mom had found love, I felt so grateful that
now I had the kind of father I didn't get the first time around. PJ
made me lunch for school, even though I was in high school and
could have been making my own. He drove me to my orthodontist
appointments because I didn't have a car. But my favorite thing?
He made dinner and served it every night at six o'clock, and we all
sat around the table to eat—together. That one thing made me the
happiest I'd been in a long time.

Rich and tender, beef stew was always a favorite in our house.
PJ would make a big pot of it, and the smell after it had simmered
for hours would hit me as I walked through the door from my shift
at the local pizzeria. This is an updated version, with rendered
bacon fat for a bit of smokiness and some tomato paste for a little
sweetness. Otherwise, I've stayed close to home with this classic, and
it's just as comforting as it was way back then.

---

1 Preheat the oven to 300°F. Pat the beef dry with paper towels
   and season the pieces evenly with the salt and pepper. Toss
   them with 2 tablespoons of the flour.

2 In a large Dutch oven, cook the bacon over medium-high
   heat until crispy, 5 to 7 minutes. Transfer to a paper towel–
   lined plate. Add half of the floured beef and cook, turning
   occasionally, until browned on all sides, about 5 minutes.
   Transfer to a plate. Add the remainder of the beef, repeat the
   cooking process, and transfer to the plate.

3 Reduce the heat slightly, add the olive oil and onion to the pot
   and cook, stirring frequently, until the onion is just softened,
   about 4 minutes. Add the garlic and cook, stirring constantly,
   until fragrant, about 30 seconds. Add the butter and cook
   until melted.

Serves 6

PER SERVING	
Calories	437
Protein	31 g
Carbohydrates	40 g
Fiber	12 g
Sugar	3 g
Total Fat	17 g
Saturated Fat	8 g
Sodium	925 mg

3 pounds boneless beef chuck
    roast, cut into 2-inch pieces
½ teaspoon salt
¼ teaspoon freshly ground
    black pepper
3 tablespoons all-purpose flour
4 slices bacon
1 tablespoon extra-virgin
    olive oil
1 large onion, chopped (about
    1¼ cups)
3 garlic cloves, minced
2 tablespoons unsalted butter
1 cup dry red wine (I like
    Burgundy)
2 cups low-sodium beef broth
1 tablespoon tomato paste
2 bay leaves
Leaves from 2 sprigs of fresh
    thyme (about 1 tablespoon)
2 tablespoons finely chopped
    fresh rosemary leaves

4 Sprinkle the remaining 1 tablespoon of flour into the pot and stir. (The flour will be clumpy.) Slowly add the wine, stirring constantly and scraping up any crispy bits on the bottom of the pot. Add the broth, tomato paste, bay leaves, thyme, and rosemary, and bring the mixture to a simmer. Return the meat to the pot and bring the mixture back to a simmer.

5 Cover the pot, transfer it to the oven, and cook for 1 hour. Remove the pot from the oven and add the potatoes, carrots, and parsnips. Cover and return the pot to the oven until the meat is tender, about 1 hour more. Crumble the cooked bacon into the pot, add the fresh parsley, stir, and serve.

4 small red potatoes, quartered (about 4 cups)

4 large carrots, cut into 1-inch pieces (about 3 cups)

2 medium parsnips, cut into 1-inch pieces (about 1½ cups)

½ cup packed chopped fresh flat-leaf parsley

LEMON CREAM RISOTTO

Risotto is one of those things I reserve for ordering at restaurants and rarely make at home. But after a few recent attempts, I've got to say it's worth every minute of the required standing and stirring. Adding cream makes an already-rich dish that much more delicious, and with the hearty dose of Pecorino Romano cheese that's an absolute must, this becomes one of the best "sometimes" meals.

    I love serving this rich risotto alongside the Lemon Roasted Chicken (page 138) in place of the Moroccan Couscous, or even as a more decadent side for the Chicken & Mushrooms in Mustard Marsala Cream Sauce (page 141).

Serves 4

PER SERVING	
Calories	682
Protein	16 g
Carbohydrates	94 g
Fiber	2 g
Sugar	1 g
Total Fat	22 g
Saturated Fat	14 g
Sodium	577 mg

6 cups low-sodium chicken broth

1 bay leaf

4 tablespoons (½ stick) unsalted butter

⅓ cup finely chopped yellow onion

2 garlic cloves, minced

2 cups Arborio rice

¼ cup dry white wine

¼ cup heavy cream

⅔ cup freshly grated Pecorino Romano cheese

2 tablespoons finely chopped fresh basil leaves

Zest and juice of 1 lemon

¼ teaspoon salt

¼ teaspoon freshly ground black pepper

1   In a large saucepan, bring the broth and bay leaf to a boil over medium-high heat. Cover, reduce the heat to low, and keep warm.

2   In a separate large saucepan, melt 3 tablespoons of the butter over medium heat. Add the onion and garlic and cook until softened, about 4 minutes.

3   Add the rice, stir to coat, and toast it, stirring constantly, for 1 minute. Add the wine and stir until evaporated, about 1 minute.

4   Add 1½ cups of the hot broth, bring to a simmer, and cook, stirring frequently, until absorbed, about 10 minutes.

5   Add the remaining broth, ½ cup at a time, stirring frequently after each addition and allowing the broth to be absorbed before adding more, until the rice is creamy and tender, 35 to 40 minutes.

6   Stir in the remaining 1 tablespoon of butter, the cream, cheese, basil, lemon zest and juice, salt, and pepper. Serve immediately.

All Things Sweet

**PEANUT BUTTER MOUSSE PIE WITH
MARSHMALLOW WHIPPED CREAM,**
page 200

PEANUT BUTTER MOUSSE
PIE WITH MARSHMALLOW
WHIPPED CREAM   200

LEMON POPPY SEED
CUPCAKES WITH VANILLA
CREAM CHEESE FROSTING   202

GOOEY CHOCOLATE CHIP
COOKIE PIE   206

LIME COCONUT CREAM CUPS   210

SKILLET APPLE CRISP WITH
WHISKEY CARAMEL SAUCE   215

MINI LEMON-RASPBERRY
CHEESECAKES WITH
CRUMBLE TOPPING   217

COCONUT OATMEAL COOKIES
WITH CARAMEL DRIZZLE   222

DULCE DE LECHE
CREAM-FILLED DOUGHNUTS
WITH CHOCOLATE GLAZE   225

PEPPERMINT COOKIES-AND-
CREAM FUDGE BROWNIES   230

CHOCOLATE HAZELNUT
BREAD PUDDING
WITH SALTED PEANUT
BUTTER SAUCE   233

PEANUT BUTTER MOUSSE PIE WITH MARSHMALLOW WHIPPED CREAM

There is one perfect sandwich from my childhood: the fluffernutter. If you're from New England, you grew up with it, too. How marshmallow fluff became an appropriate sandwich filling, I'll never know, but I'm so glad it did. It's the best partner for peanut butter, and I don't care what anyone says about jelly. This pie combines everything I love about a fluffernutter and more: a salty pretzel crust, creamy peanut butter filling, and a marshmallow whipped cream.

1 For the pretzel crust, preheat the oven to 375°F.

2 In the bowl of a food processor, pulse the pretzels and peanuts to fine crumbs. You may have to do this in 2 batches.

3 Transfer to a bowl and stir in the confectioners' sugar. Add the melted butter and stir well. Press into the bottom and up the sides of a 9-inch pie plate.

4 Bake the crust until set, about 10 minutes. Let cool completely on a wire rack.

5 For the peanut butter mousse, in the bowl of a stand mixer fitted with the whisk attachment, beat the heavy cream and vanilla on medium-high speed until stiff peaks form, about 2 minutes. Transfer to a small bowl.

6 Fit the paddle attachment onto the mixer and beat the cream cheese and peanut butter on medium speed until blended. Add the sugar and beat until smooth.

Serves 10

PER SERVING	
Calories	745
Protein	13 g
Carbohydrates	57 g
Fiber	3 g
Sugar	33 g
Total Fat	54 g
Saturated Fat	26 g
Sodium	596 mg

Crust

7 ounces salted pretzels (about 4 cups)

½ cup dry-roasted unsalted peanuts

¼ cup confectioners' sugar

8 tablespoons (1 stick) unsalted butter, melted

Peanut Butter Mousse

8 ounces cream cheese, at room temperature

1 cup creamy (*not* natural) peanut butter

¾ cup confectioners' sugar

1¼ cups heavy cream

1 teaspoon pure vanilla extract

7 Using a rubber spatula, fold the whipped cream into the peanut butter mixture until smooth. Spread the peanut butter mousse into the cooled pretzel crust and smooth the top.

8 For the marshmallow whipped cream, in the bowl of a stand mixer fitted with the whisk attachment, beat the heavy cream, vanilla, and granulated sugar on medium-high speed until stiff peaks form, about 2 minutes.

9 Add the marshmallow fluff in two additions, beating after each one, until fully incorporated, fluffy, and glossy, about 2 minutes.

10 Spread the topping over the pie, leaving a 1-inch border of the peanut butter mousse exposed. Sprinkle the marshmallow topping with the chocolate shavings.

11 Chill for at least 2 hours before serving. Any leftover pie will keep, covered, in the refrigerator for up to 4 days.

Marshmallow Whipped Cream

1 cup heavy cream

1 teaspoon pure vanilla extract

¼ cup granulated sugar

2 cups (7-ounce jar) marshmallow fluff

2 ounces 70% dark chocolate, coarsely shaved, for topping

LEMON POPPY SEED CUPCAKES WITH VANILLA CREAM CHEESE FROSTING

My aunt Maureen used to buy all of us kids mini lemon poppy seed muffins for breakfast when I stayed over her house in the summer, and they were just the lightest, most delicious little things. My lemon poppy seed cupcakes remind me of those sweet and faintly tart little muffins. These, though, are full-size cupcakes, and I whipped up a grown-up frosting using a real vanilla bean to give them a bit more class.

Makes 1 dozen

PER CUPCAKE	
Calories	520
Protein	5 g
Carbohydrates	66 g
Fiber	1 g
Sugar	50 g
Total Fat	27 g
Saturated Fat	16 g
Sodium	225 mg

1½ cups all-purpose flour

1¾ teaspoons baking powder

½ teaspoon salt

10 tablespoons (1¼ sticks) unsalted butter, at room temperature

1 cup sugar

2 large eggs

½ cup sour cream

¼ cup fresh lemon juice

2 tablespoons grated lemon zest (about 1 lemon)

1 teaspoon pure vanilla extract

2 tablespoons poppy seeds

Vanilla Cream Cheese Frosting (recipe follows)

1 Preheat the oven to 350°F. Line a standard cupcake tin with paper liners.

2 In a medium bowl, whisk together the flour, baking powder, and salt.

3 In the bowl of a stand mixer fitted with the paddle attachment, beat the butter and sugar at medium-high speed until fluffy, about 3 minutes. Add the eggs and beat until incorporated, about 1 minute. Add the sour cream, lemon juice, lemon zest, vanilla, and poppy seeds.

4 With the mixer on low speed, gradually add the flour mixture, beating just until combined, about 1 minute. Be careful not to overmix. The batter will be thick. Spoon it evenly into the prepared tin.

5 Bake until a toothpick inserted into the center of a cupcake comes out clean or with a few moist crumbs attached, 16 to 20 minutes. Let the cupcakes cool for 2 minutes in the cupcake tin, then carefully turn them out of the tin and let cool completely on a wire rack.

6 Frost with the Vanilla Cream Cheese Frosting. The cupcakes will keep in an airtight container in the refrigerator for 4 days.

PER ⅛ CUP	
Calories	107
Protein	1 g
Carbohydrates	12 g
Fiber	0 g
Sugar	11 g
Total Fat	7 g
Saturated Fat	4 g
Sodium	32 mg

Vanilla Cream Cheese Frosting

Makes about 2 cups; 16 servings

6 ounces cream cheese, at room temperature

4 tablespoons (½ stick) unsalted butter

2 vanilla beans

1½ cups confectioners' sugar

1 tablespoon whole milk

1   Put the cream cheese and butter in the bowl of a stand mixer fitted with the whisk attachment. Using a paring knife, halve the vanilla beans lengthwise and scrape the seeds into the bowl. Beat on medium speed until the cream cheese and butter are combined and creamy and the vanilla seeds are mixed throughout, about 1 minute.

2   Gradually add the confectioners' sugar, 1 cup at a time, and beat on medium-high speed until incorporated. Scrape down the sides of the bowl, increase the mixer speed to high, and beat until completely smooth, about 2 minutes. Add the milk and beat for 1 minute more.

GOOEY CHOCOLATE CHIP
COOKIE PIE

I fell in love with Derby Pie years ago, and this recipe pays tribute to that gooey masterpiece. It's a marriage of perfectly chewy chocolate chip cookies and pie. What could be better than flaky pie crust with buttery chocolate-and-walnut-studded filling? Nothing.

----

1 For the crust, in a food processor, combine the flour, sugar, and salt. Add the butter and pulse until the mixture is crumbly and the pieces of butter are roughly the size of small peas, 4 to 5 pulses.

2 Transfer the mixture to a large bowl. Add the ice water and use a rubber spatula or a large spoon to fold the water into the mixture until a dough forms. Pat the dough into a ball, turn it out onto a sheet of plastic wrap, and flatten into a 4-inch disk. Wrap it tightly and refrigerate for at least 30 minutes and up to 2 days.

3 Remove the dough from the refrigerator and let stand at room temperature for 15 minutes. On a clean, lightly floured work surface, roll the dough out into a 12-inch circle. Transfer to a 9-inch pie plate and press it into the bottom and up the sides.

4 Trim the overhang to ½ inch beyond the lip of the plate and tuck the remainder under itself. Use your fingers to pinch the dough, crimping the edges evenly. Cover the pie loosely with plastic wrap and refrigerate while you make the filling.

5 Preheat the oven to 350°F.

recipe continues

Serves 10

PER SERVING

Calories	597
Protein	9 g
Carbohydrates	60 g
Fiber	2 g
Sugar	38 g
Total Fat	37 g
Saturated Fat	18 g
Sodium	283 mg

Crust

1¼ cups all-purpose flour

1 tablespoon sugar

½ teaspoon salt

10 tablespoons (1¼ sticks) unsalted butter, cold, cut into ¼-inch pieces

4 tablespoons ice water

6   For the filling, in a small bowl, stir together the melted butter and the bourbon.

7   In a large bowl, whisk together the granulated sugar, brown sugar, flour, and salt. Whisk in the eggs until smooth. Slowly whisk in the butter-bourbon mixture. Fold in the walnuts and chocolate. Pour into the chilled pie shell.

8   Bake until the filling is slightly puffed and the center is set, 40 to 45 minutes. Let cool completely before serving with ice cream. The pie will keep, covered, in the refrigerator, for up to 3 days.

Filling

8 tablespoons (1 stick) unsalted butter, melted
3 tablespoons bourbon
1 cup granulated sugar
⅓ cup packed light brown sugar
½ cup all-purpose flour
½ teaspoon salt
2 large eggs
1 cup unsalted walnuts, toasted and chopped
3 ounces bittersweet chocolate, chopped

1½ pints vanilla ice cream, for serving

LIME COCONUT CREAM CUPS

On certain weeknights after dinner during my early teens, if we were really feeling needy, Mom and I would make homemade pudding. Tapioca, butterscotch, vanilla—though, strangely, never chocolate. We'd stand there in the kitchen with only the low light of the microwave beating down on the stovetop, and we'd stir it. Something that'd generally be considered such a chore—the endless stirring—was somehow made lovely when we did it together. We'd talk in a more meandering way than we might if we were sitting across from each other at dinner. It was as plain as a Tuesday, but still the memory stays with me. These cream cups remind me of the custards we made, though now I've taken to adding graham crumbs to give them a little delicious texture.

Serves 8

PER SERVING	
Calories	499
Protein	5 g
Carbohydrates	36 g
Fiber	1 g
Sugar	24 g
Total Fat	38 g
Saturated Fat	26 g
Sodium	184 mg

Graham Crumbs

8 whole graham crackers, crushed

2 tablespoons granulated sugar

6 tablespoons (¾ stick) unsalted butter, melted

Lime Coconut Cream

1 14-ounce can full-fat coconut milk

1 cup whole milk

½ cup sweetened shredded coconut

1 teaspoon pure vanilla extract

¼ teaspoon salt

½ cup granulated sugar

¼ cup cornstarch

6 large egg yolks

3 tablespoons unsalted butter

2 teaspoons grated lime zest

1   For the graham crumbs, preheat the oven to 325°F. Line a large rimmed baking sheet with parchment paper.

2   In a large bowl, combine the graham cracker crumbs and sugar. Add the butter and stir to moisten all the crumbs.

3   Spread the mixture on the prepared baking sheet and bake, stirring halfway, until golden brown and crisp, about 10 minutes. Let cool completely on a wire rack. Divide the crumbs among 8 small ramekins or glass jars.

4   For the lime coconut cream, in a medium saucepan set over medium-high heat, combine the coconut milk, whole milk, shredded coconut, vanilla, and salt, and bring to a simmer.

5   In a medium bowl, whisk together the granulated sugar and cornstarch. Whisk in the egg yolks.

6 Slowly whisk 1 cup of the hot coconut milk mixture into the egg yolk mixture, then slowly whisk the now-warmed yolk mixture back into the saucepan of simmering milk. Reduce the heat to medium and cook, whisking constantly, until the mixture has thickened, 1 to 2 minutes.

7 Remove the pan from the heat and whisk in the butter and lime zest. Let the pudding cool, stirring frequently, for about 10 minutes. Pour the pudding over the graham crumbs in the ramekins and refrigerate until chilled and set, about 4 hours.

8 For the topping, preheat the oven to 325°F. On a large baking sheet lined with parchment paper, spread the shredded coconut in an even layer and bake, stirring halfway, until lightly golden and fragrant, 6 to 8 minutes.

9 In the bowl of a stand mixer fitted with the whisk attachment, beat the cream, confectioners' sugar, and vanilla on medium-high speed until stiff peaks form, 1 to 2 minutes.

10 To serve, top each coconut cream cup with a dollop of whipped cream and a sprinkling of toasted coconut.

Topping

½ cup sweetened shredded coconut
½ cup heavy cream
2 tablespoons confectioners' sugar
½ teaspoon pure vanilla extract

SKILLET APPLE CRISP WITH WHISKEY CARAMEL SAUCE

Every year, my mom and I have an hour-long phone conversation about what we'll serve at Thanksgiving dinner. "Okay, so for pies...," she'll start the list, "Cranberry walnut, blueberry, pumpkin white chocolate cheesecake, coconut custard..." She trails off.

"Will that be enough for six of us?" She's not joking when she asks this. I smile a small smile and sigh quietly as I tell her yes, it's plenty. We hadn't even yet talked about the two apple pies she'd make because they're almost too obvious; we couldn't have Thanksgiving without them, and Mom prides herself on her apple pie.

Now, I love my mom's pie more than anything, but I don't always love the fuss of making pie dough. Instead, I like to make this skillet recipe with a buttery crisp topping. It offers all the gooey warmth and richness of pie in half the time.

1 Preheat the oven to 425°F.

2 For the topping, in a large bowl, whisk together the flour, oats, brown sugar, and salt. Using a fork or a pastry blender, work the butter into the flour mixture until a crumbly topping is formed.

3 In a large bowl, toss the apples with the granulated sugar, brown sugar, cinnamon, and nutmeg.

4 In a 12-inch ovenproof or cast-iron skillet, melt the butter over medium heat. Add the apple mixture and cook, stirring frequently, until the apples are just beginning to soften, about 12 minutes.

recipe continues

Serves 10

PER SERVING

Calories	546
Protein	3 g
Carbohydrates	79 g
Fiber	3 g
Sugar	64 g
Total Fat	26 g
Saturated Fat	16 g
Sodium	150 mg

Topping

¾ cup all-purpose flour

¾ cup old-fashioned rolled oats

¾ cup packed light brown sugar

¾ teaspoon ground cinnamon

½ teaspoon salt

8 tablespoons (1 stick) unsalted butter, at room temperature

Apples

4 pounds Honeycrisp apples, peeled, cored, and cut into ½-inch-thick slices

¼ cup granulated sugar

¼ cup packed light brown sugar

1 teaspoon ground cinnamon

¼ teaspoon ground nutmeg

2 tablespoons unsalted butter

5 Sprinkle the topping evenly over the apples, place the skillet on a baking sheet, and bake until the apples are tender and the topping is golden brown, 18 to 20 minutes.

6 Transfer the skillet to a wire rack and let cool for 10 to 15 minutes before serving.

7 For the whiskey caramel sauce, in a small saucepan, melt the butter. Add the brown sugar and cook, stirring occasionally, until the sugar is dissolved and the mixture is smooth, 2 to 3 minutes.

8 Bring to a boil, reduce the heat to medium-low, and let the sauce simmer until it is a deep golden brown, 2 to 3 minutes.

9 Remove the pan from the heat and slowly whisk in the heavy cream. Whisk in the vanilla and whiskey. Transfer the caramel to a small bowl.

10 Serve the apple crisp warm with the whiskey caramel sauce on the side so that guests can drizzle it over their servings. Leftover apple crisp will keep, covered, in the refrigerator, for up to 3 days. Leftover caramel sauce will keep, covered, in the refrigerator, for up to 2 weeks.

Whiskey Caramel Sauce

8 tablespoons (1 stick) unsalted butter
1 cup packed light brown sugar
½ teaspoon pure vanilla extract
½ cup heavy cream
2 tablespoons whiskey

MINI LEMON-RASPBERRY CHEESECAKES WITH CRUMBLE TOPPING

Crumbles and crisps are the most crowd pleasing of desserts. What's not to love? Syrupy-sweet fruit and a crunchy topping—gets me every time. This one takes the crumble up a notch—with a quick lemon cheesecake bottom. The lemony layer, coupled with a sweet-tart raspberry filling and a buttery almond topping, is refreshing and summery.

1 Preheat the oven to 325°F. Place eight 8-ounce ramekins in a high-sided roasting pan.

2 For the crust, in the bowl of a food processor, pulse the graham crackers and sugar until finely ground, about 4 pulses. Transfer the crumbs to a medium bowl and stir in the melted butter, continuing to stir until the crumbs are well coated.

3 Press the crumbs into the bottom of each ramekin. Bake until the crusts are fragrant and light golden brown, 6 to 8 minutes. Let cool slightly and transfer the ramekins to a large baking dish with high sides.

4 For the filling, in the bowl of a stand mixer fitted with the paddle attachment, beat the cream cheese and 2/3 cup of the sugar. Add the eggs, lemon zest and juice, heavy cream, and vanilla, and continue beating on medium speed just until blended, about 1 minute. Divide the cheesecake mixture among the ramekins.

5 In a medium bowl, toss the raspberries with the remaining 3 tablespoons of sugar. Set aside while you make the topping.

recipe continues

Serves 8

PER SERVING	
Calories	487
Protein	8 g
Carbohydrates	52 g
Fiber	4 g
Sugar	41 g
Total Fat	29 g
Saturated Fat	17 g
Sodium	190 mg

Crust

8 whole graham crackers, broken into large pieces

3 tablespoons sugar

4 tablespoons (½ stick) unsalted butter, melted

Filling

16 ounces (2 packages) cream cheese, at room temperature

2/3 cup plus 3 tablespoons sugar

2 large eggs

2 tablespoons grated lemon zest (about 2 lemons)

2 tablespoons fresh lemon juice

3 tablespoons heavy cream

1 teaspoon pure vanilla extract

2½ cups fresh raspberries

6   For the topping, in another medium bowl, whisk together the flour and brown sugar. Using a fork or a pastry blender, work the butter into the flour mixture until a crumbly dough is formed.

7   Top each ramekin with the raspberries. Scatter the crumble topping evenly over top of the raspberries and sprinkle with the sliced almonds. Pour boiling water into the roasting pan until it reaches halfway up the sides of the ramekins.

8   Bake until the topping is golden brown and the berries are bubbling around the sides of the ramekins, 25 to 30 minutes. Carefully remove the ramekins from the water bath and let cool on a wire rack. Serve warm, at room temperature, or chilled.

Crumble Topping

⅓ cup all-purpose flour

⅓ cup packed light brown sugar

4 tablespoons (½ stick) unsalted butter, room temperature

¼ cup sliced unsalted almonds

I'LL NEVER GIVE UP CAKE

* ❁ *

My mother is the one person I cannot imagine living without. She's my best friend. And if I were to find the right language to explain it, I'd have to do some math: Multiply love by infinity, and then take that to the tenth power. When I went away to college, to Italy, and then away to various states, each move felt like I was taking off another piece of clothing—I was so vulnerable. I missed her. I wanted to crawl inside that spot between her earlobe and the base of her neck, where it smells like Clinique Happy and reassurance.

At the end of 2011, when I signed my book deals, I called her.

"Oh, baby," she said, choking back tears. "We've got to celebrate. I'll go to White's Bakery."

And with that, she hung up the phone, swiped Dee Dee from her pug post beside the living room window, and drove forty minutes down to Hingham, Massachusetts. The engine of my mother's Corolla, I imagine, ferociously purring at thirty-four miles an hour.

Days later and many conversations in between, I arrived home to find a box. She had mailed me my favorite cake in the world. The tenderest, most perfect double-layer white cake, now smashed to mush inside a cardboard box.

I called her. "Mama, wow!"

"Baby, you got the cake?!"

"Yes and I love it so much. I love it so, so much."

"Did it hold up?"

I peek at the mess inside the box, nothing more than a frosting cake mash. I smiled. "It's perfect."

Ten years ago, I had quit cake—all desserts. I was on a mission to lose weight, and I just knew, really knew, that I couldn't have one sliver of cake without that sliver turning to two, to three, to . . . The whole thirteen months in which I lost more than one hundred pounds was intensely challenging. I missed cake the way I would miss my friend if she moved away to Singapore indefinitely. *How soon will she be back?*

At first, I tried to lighten the desserts I loved. I traded the real ingredients for sugar substitutes, butter substitutes, and the worst-tasting ingredient of all: fat-free cream cheese. My mom would try them, her smile as fake as the taste of aspartame. I learned the hard way that most of my efforts at lightening tended to, ironically enough, result in a leaden dessert. And worse, I realized that I wasn't satisfied after eating them. I binged on the lighter versions, eating just as many calories as I might have if I had made the real deal—only this time by having three servings. My itch for real cupcakes, real brownies was still there, unscratched by these lighter sweets.

I gave up.

I made a promise to myself right then and there that if I was going to have dessert, I was going to do it right and truly enjoy it.

When my mom mailed me that cake from thousands of miles across the country, to celebrate the books, I opened that banged-up box. It had been a year since I'd last had a cake from my favorite bakery, and here it was, all mine. Ten years prior to that moment, I might have grabbed a fork and dug in without even considering a plate or a portion or how I'd feel about myself when I was done. Now, I scooped some of that cake mash into a dish, sat down at my table, and enjoyed every celebratory bite with Daniel. Then I portioned the rest of the cake into smaller containers to enjoy every so often, when I needed a treat, or a taste of home.

For me, dessert is just one more way I connect to the love of my life: my mother. Eating certain sweets is a jog back to a day in our first kitchen, when I learned patience and care through baking. I love knowing that my sweet tooth is hers, too, and for that, I don't wish it away, even when it aches.

The things we look forward to in life—like desserts and parties and vacations—they're special because they don't happen every day. And they're shared.

Make it special, I always tell myself when I consider dessert. *Only eat sweets that you truly love*, I say.

COCONUT OATMEAL COOKIES WITH CARAMEL DRIZZLE

A normal human being knows that a visit to the dentist is not an event that merits sugary treats. But for me and my family—none of whom is a normal human being—it always includes baking up a dessert to give to the staff. These cookies were what I brought to my last cleaning, and they were the most raved-about baked good to date. They're ultra chewy and soft in the center, laced with coconut, and studded with walnuts and chocolate chips. I suggest baking them for anyone you need a favor from—including, but not limited to, your dentist.

1   Preheat the oven to 350°F. Line 2 large rimmed baking sheets with parchment paper.

2   In a medium bowl, whisk together the flour, baking powder, baking soda, and salt.

3   In a separate medium bowl, combine the oats, walnuts, coconut, and chocolate chips.

4   In the bowl of a stand mixer fitted with the paddle attachment, beat the butter and brown sugar on medium-high speed until smooth, about 3 minutes. Add the egg and vanilla and beat to incorporate.

5   With the mixer running on low speed, gradually add the flour mixture and beat until just combined. Stir in the oat mixture. Be careful not to overmix.

6   Scoop out 2 level tablespoons of dough per cookie and place them 2 inches apart on the prepared baking sheets, Using your hands, gently flatten the balls.

recipe continues

Makes 36; serves 36

PER COOKIE

Calories	163
Protein	2 g
Carbohydrates	20 g
Fiber	1 g
Sugar	13 g
Total Fat	9 g
Saturated Fat	4 g
Sodium	76 mg

Cookies

1¼ cups all-purpose flour

¾ teaspoon baking powder

½ teaspoon baking soda

½ teaspoon salt

2 cups old-fashioned rolled oats

1 cup unsalted walnuts, toasted and chopped

1 cup sweetened shredded coconut

¾ cup semisweet chocolate chips

10 tablespoons (1¼ sticks) unsalted butter, at room temperature

1¼ cups packed dark brown sugar

1 large egg

2 teaspoons pure vanilla extract

7   Bake, rotating the baking sheets halfway, front to back and top to bottom, until the cookies are golden, the edges are crisp, and the centers are still soft and underdone, 13 to 15 minutes. Let cool completely on the baking sheets before transferring to a wire rack.

8   For the caramel drizzle, in a small microwave-safe bowl, combine the caramels and cream. Microwave on high, stirring after every minute, until the caramels are melted and the mixture is smooth, 1 to 2 minutes. Drizzle over the cookies. Let cool completely until the caramel is set. The cookies will keep in an airtight container at room temperature for up to 1 week.

Caramel Drizzle

12 soft caramels, unwrapped
2 tablespoons heavy cream

DULCE DE LECHE CREAM-FILLED DOUGHNUTS WITH CHOCOLATE GLAZE

My mom makes the best pecan pie I've ever had. She also loves doughnuts with a ferocity second only to mine. The wild abandon of this recipe—just the sheer decadence—feels so right when I think of her. She's the type who always suggests adding more sugar, more butter, a splash more cream. "Too much" is just her standard operating mode.

---

1 For the doughnuts, in the bowl of a stand mixer fitted with the paddle attachment, combine the milk and yeast and mix on low speed until foamy, about 3 minutes.

2 In a large bowl, whisk together the flour, sugar, salt, and cinnamon. Add to the yeast mixture and mix until combined.

3 Add the egg and mix until just incorporated.

4 Add the butter and mix until combined. Increase the mixer speed to medium and mix the dough until it is smooth and slightly sticky, and begins to pull away from the side of the bowl, about 5 minutes.

5 Remove the dough from the mixer, form it into a smooth ball, and place it in a large bowl coated with a thin layer of oil. Cover the bowl with plastic wrap and let the dough rise in a warm area until it has almost tripled in size, about 30 minutes.

6 Turn the dough out onto a clean, lightly floured surface. Lightly flour the top of the dough and use a rolling pin to roll it into a ½-inch-thick disk. Use a 2½- or 3-inch biscuit cutter to cut 12 doughnut rounds.

recipe continues

Makes 12; serves 12

PER SERVING	
Calories	575
Protein	7 g
Carbohydrates	43 g
Fiber	2 g
Sugar	26 g
Fat	42 g
Saturated Fat	17 g
Sodium	278 mg

Doughnuts

1¼ cups whole milk, warmed

3 teaspoons active dry yeast

3½ cups all-purpose flour, plus more for dusting

3 tablespoons sugar

1 teaspoon salt

1½ teaspoons ground cinnamon

1 large egg

6 tablespoons (¾ stick) unsalted butter, at room temperature

Canola oil, for frying

Chocolate Glaze (recipe follows)
Candied Pecans (recipe follows)

7   In a large, heavy-bottomed pot set over medium-high heat, heat the canola oil until it reaches 350°F on a candy thermometer. Working in batches, carefully drop the dough into the hot oil and fry until golden brown, about 90 seconds per side.

8   Use a slotted spoon to transfer the doughnuts to a paper towel–lined plate and let cool completely.

9   For the dulce de leche filling, in the bowl of a stand mixer fitted with the paddle attachment, cream the butter and cream cheese on medium speed until smooth. Add the dulce de leche and beat until completely incorporated. Add the confectioners' sugar, one cup at a time, scraping down the sides of the bowl as needed, and beat until smooth, about 2 minutes. If not using immediately, store the filling in the refrigerator until ready to use. The filling will keep, covered, in the refrigerator for up to 3 days. If chilled, allow it to soften slightly at room temperature and re-beat before filling the doughnuts.

10 To finish the cooled doughnuts, poke a small hole in the side of each doughnut using a chopstick. Fit a pastry bag with a small round tip (#2) and fill the bag with the pastry cream.

11 Inserting the tip of the pastry bag into each doughnut hole, squeeze 3 to 4 tablespoons of the filling inside. Dip the tops of the doughnuts into the chocolate glaze and, while the chocolate is still wet, sprinkle the tops with the candied pecans.

Dulce de Leche Filling

4 tablespoons unsalted butter, at room temperature

8 ounces cream cheese, at room temperature

⅓ cup store-bought dulce de leche

3 cups confectioners' sugar

PER 1 TBSP	
Calories	80
Protein	1 g
Carbohydrates	8 g
Fiber	0 g
Sugar	7 g
Total Fat	6 g
Saturated Fat	3 g
Sodium	5 mg

Chocolate Glaze
Makes 1 cup

¼ cup heavy cream

2 tablespoons light corn syrup

4 ounces semisweet chocolate, finely chopped

1 teaspoon pure vanilla extract

3 tablespoons unsalted butter

3 tablespoons confectioners' sugar

1 In a small saucepan set over medium heat, combine the heavy cream and corn syrup and cook, whisking constantly, until the corn syrup has dissolved into the cream, 1 to 2 minutes.

2 Reduce the heat to medium-low, whisk in the chocolate and vanilla, and cook, whisking constantly, until the chocolate has melted, about 2 minutes.

3 Remove the pan from the heat and whisk in the butter until smooth. Whisk in the confectioners' sugar until smooth.

4 Use immediately, while warm. To keep the glaze warm, place it in a heatproof bowl set on top of (not in) a pot of simmering water, and stir occasionally to keep it from burning.

PER 1 TBSP	
Calories	89
Protein	1 g
Carbohydrates	4 g
Fiber	1 g
Sugar	4 g
Total Fat	8 g
Saturated Fat	2 g
Sodium	38 mg

Candied Pecans
Makes ½ cup

2 tablespoons unsalted butter

2 tablespoons packed light brown sugar

¼ teaspoon ground cinnamon

⅛ teaspoon salt

½ cup unsalted pecans, toasted and chopped

_____

1 Line a large rimmed baking sheet with wax paper.

2 In a 10-inch nonstick skillet set over medium heat, melt the butter. Add the sugar, cinnamon, and salt, and cook, stirring, until the sugar has begun to dissolve, about 1 minute.

3 Add the pecans, toss to coat, and cook until the glaze is sticky and slightly thickened, about 1 minute.

4 Spread the pecans on the prepared baking sheet. Let cool completely, 45 minutes to 1 hour. The pecans can be made up to 2 days ahead and stored in an airtight container at room temperature.

PEPPERMINT COOKIES-AND-CREAM FUDGE BROWNIES

When I want something supremely chocolaty, there's nothing that satisfies like a big honking fudge brownie. Except maybe a big honking fudge brownie topped with light-as-air peppermint cookies-and-cream frosting. And don't pigeonhole peppermint desserts as Christmas desserts! They are delicious enough to be enjoyed any time of year.

1 For the brownies, preheat the oven to 350°F. Grease a 9 × 13-inch baking dish.

2 In a medium bowl, whisk together the flour, baking powder, and salt.

3 In a small saucepan set over medium heat, melt the butter and chocolate. Pour the mixture into a large bowl and let it cool slightly, about 5 minutes. Add the granulated and brown sugars and whisk until smooth. Whisk in the eggs and vanilla. Stir in the flour mixture until just combined. Pour the batter into the prepared pan.

4 Bake until a toothpick inserted in the center comes out with a few crumbs, 30 to 35 minutes. Cool completely in the pan on a wire rack.

5 For the frosting, in the bowl of a stand mixer fitted with the whisk attachment, beat the butter. Gradually add the confectioners' sugar and beat on medium-high speed until incorporated, about 2 minutes. Add the peppermint extract and cream and beat on high speed until light and fluffy, about 2 more minutes. Stir in the crushed Oreos.

recipe continues

Makes 24; serves 24

PER SERVING	
Calories	323
Protein	3 g
Carbohydrates	42 g
Fiber	1 g
Sugar	33 g
Total Fat	18 g
Saturated Fat	10 g
Sodium	96 mg

Brownies
1 cup all-purpose flour

¾ teaspoon baking powder

½ teaspoon salt

10 tablespoons (1½ sticks) unsalted butter

6 ounces unsweetened baking chocolate, chopped

1 cup granulated sugar

1 cup packed light brown sugar

3 large eggs

1 teaspoon pure vanilla extract

Frosting
8 tablespoons (1 stick) unsalted butter, at room temperature

3 cups confectioners' sugar, sifted

¼ teaspoon peppermint extract

¼ cup heavy cream

10 Oreo cookies, crushed

6   For the ganache, place the chocolate chips in a medium bowl.

7   In a small saucepan, bring the heavy cream to a simmer over medium-high heat. Pour the hot cream over the chocolate chips and let stand for 5 minutes to allow the chocolate to melt. Stir until the chocolate is smooth and glossy. Let the ganache cool, stirring occasionally, until it reaches room temperature.

8   Frost the cooled brownies, using a butter knife or an offset spatula, then drizzle the ganache over top. Cut into 24 squares and serve. Leftovers will keep in an airtight container in the refrigerator for up to 4 days.

Ganache

1 cup semisweet chocolate chips

½ cup heavy cream

CHOCOLATE HAZELNUT BREAD PUDDING WITH SALTED PEANUT BUTTER SAUCE

I have one rule with bread pudding: it cannot, in any way, be dry or even crisp on top. No, I want softness—for the bread to be fully puffed with creamy custard. This recipe delivers in every way. A hazelnut-chocolate custard cooks right into fluffy challah bread cubes, and then the whole thing gets drizzled with a rich, salty peanut butter sauce. Serve it warm, and don't concern yourself with how to store leftovers, because there won't be any.

1 Preheat the oven to 325°F. Grease a 9 × 13-inch baking dish. Spread the bread cubes, chocolate chips, and hazelnuts in the dish.

2 In a medium microwave-safe bowl, microwave the chopped chocolate until melted, 1 to 2 minutes, stirring after every 30 seconds to prevent burning.

3 In a large heatproof bowl, whisk together the eggs, sugar, vanilla, and salt.

4 In a medium saucepan, bring the milk and cream to a simmer over medium heat. While whisking constantly, slowly pour the hot cream and milk into the egg mixture. Whisk in the melted chocolate. Pour the custard over the bread cubes, taking care to cover all of them evenly. Press the bread cubes gently into the custard.

5 Bake until the custard is just set and pressing the center of the pudding with a finger shows no signs of runny liquid, 45 to 50 minutes. Transfer to a wire rack and let cool for 30 minutes.

recipe continues

Serves 12

PER SERVING	
Calories	691
Protein	16 g
Carbohydrates	66 g
Fiber	4 g
Sugar	47 g
Total Fat	43 g
Saturated Fat	18 g
Sodium	550 mg

Bread Pudding

1 16-ounce loaf of challah bread, cut into 1-inch pieces (about 12 cups)

½ cup semisweet chocolate chips

1 cup toasted unsalted hazelnuts, chopped

10 ounces semisweet chocolate, chopped

6 large eggs

1 cup granulated sugar

2 teaspoons pure vanilla extract

½ teaspoon salt

3 cups whole milk

1¼ cups heavy cream

6   For the salted peanut butter sauce, in a small saucepan, heat
    the butter and brown sugar over medium heat until the butter
    is melted and the sugar has dissolved. Add the peanut butter
    and salt and cook, whisking constantly, until the mixture is
    smooth. Remove the pan from the heat and whisk in the heavy
    cream until smooth.

7   Serve the bread pudding warm with the salted peanut butter
    sauce. Leftover bread pudding will keep, covered, in the
    refrigerator for up to 3 days. Cover and store any remaining
    peanut butter sauce in the refrigerator for up to 1 week.

Salted Peanut Butter Sauce

3 tablespoons unsalted butter
3 tablespoons packed light
   brown sugar
¾ cup creamy (not natural)
   peanut butter
¾ teaspoon salt
3 tablespoons heavy cream

ACKNOWLEDGMENTS

* 🌸 *

Thank you, forever and always, to all of the readers of CanYouStayforDinner.com. It's you who I wrote this book for.

Ashley Phillips Meyer, thank you for being my editor and dear friend. You made this book come to life. I couldn't have done it without you. Doris Cooper, thank you for taking a chance on me. Your enthusiasm feels better than anything I eat. Seriously. Erica Gelbard Callahan, you're like family. Thank you for every precious minute you put into our books. Our friendship is so special. Carly Gorga, thank you for working so hard and making me laugh the whole way through. Danielle Deschenes, thank you for your incredible vision. Terry Deal, thank you for your incredible attention to detail. And to all of the other kind, generous, and hardworking people at Clarkson Potter and Penguin Random House who took part in making this book, I am so grateful. Thank you thank you thank you.

Aran Goyoaga, this book is beautiful because of you and your gorgeous photographs. I can't begin to thank you. I'm so proud to call you my friend.

Jenn Elliott Blake, your style is out of this world. Thank you for your attention to detail, your impeccable taste, and for that insane prop collection. Getting to know you was a complete bonus. Jessie Blount, thank you for all the hours you spent cooking the recipes for these photos. You made each one look delicious.

Steve Troha, thank you for your love and dedication. You are so much more to me than my agent and you make all of our projects worthwhile.

Mom, you are the joy and the love of my life. Thank you for being you. PJ, I'll never be able to thank you for what you've meant to me. I love you. Anthony and Claire Mitchell, I love you so much. Victoria Mitchell, you're the bright spot in my life, sweet girl, and I can't wait to watch you grow.

Daniel Woolson, thank you for teaching me to trust myself and for always encouraging me to be myself. You are the best thing that ever happened to me. Kate Fernandes, Sabrina Peduto, and Nicole Loiacono, I love you with all my heart. You are my chosen family. Katie Loiacono and Caroline Loiacono, I love being able to call you my sisters. I love you.

To all of my family—especially the Deweys—and all of my friends, thank you always. I love you.

INDEX

* 🌺

A

Apple(s)
ginger apple compote, 159
shredded Brussels sprouts salad with bacon, Gorgonzola and, 87
skillet apple crisp with whiskey caramel sauce, 215–16
turkey burgers with caramelized onion, goat cheese and, 146–47

Artichoke, spinach, and sun-dried tomato omelet, creamy, 38

Arugula with orange segments, spiced walnuts and goat cheese, 84

Asian chicken salad, 57

Avocado
crema, brown sugar and chili-rubbed salmon with, 113–14
jerk shrimp salad with mango and, 109

B

Bacon
bacon-wrapped pork tenderloin with ginger apple compote, 157–59
cauliflower with, 99
meatloaf burgers with pepper Jack, frizzled onions, and, 169–70
shredded Brussels sprouts salad with apple, Gorgonzola and, 87
sweet potato hash, 43
twice-baked breakfast potatoes, 40–41

Bagel and lox salad, 64–65

Bananas
baked banana bread doughnuts with maple-cinnamon cream cheese glaze, 16–17
peanut butter granola parfaits, 34

Barbecue chicken pie, Cheddar biscuit-topped, 187–88

Basil
cashew and basil chicken lettuce wraps, 160
mashed sweet potatoes with orange zest and, 95
tuna and orzo salad with Parmesan and, 58

Beans
beef puttanesca with garlic bread, 133–34
loaded black bean burgers, 54–55
loaded chorizo nachos, 189–91
ribollita, 53
sesame green beans, 103
tuna and orzo salad with, 58
the ultimate beef chili, 66
white, creamy farro with kale and, 122

Beef
chili, ultimate, 66
meatloaf burgers with bacon, pepper Jack and frizzled onions, 169–70
PJ's meatballs and sauce, 173–74
puttanesca, with garlic bread, 133–34
spice-rubbed steak with grilled peaches and blue cheese, 163
stew, 192–93

Black bean burgers, loaded, 54–55

Blood orange mint salsa, 27

Blue cheese. See also Gorgonzola
baked buffalo chicken egg rolls, 72
spice-rubbed steak with grilled peaches and, 163

Bok choy, spicy tofu stir-fry with, 115–17

Bread pudding, chocolate hazelnut, with salted peanut butter sauce, 233–35

Breakfast, 14–43
about, 28–29
recipe list, 15

Broccoli, perfect roasted, 100

Brownies, peppermint cookies-and-cream fudge, 230–32

Brussels sprouts
coconut curry Brussels sprouts, 96
shredded, with bacon, apple and Gorgonzola, 87
spaghetti with pancetta cream and, 145

Buffalo chicken egg rolls, baked, 72

Burgers
black bean, loaded, 54–55
meatloaf, with bacon, pepper Jack and frizzled onions, 169–70
turkey, with apple, caramelized onion and goat cheese, 146–47

Buttermilk ranch dressing, 150

Butternut squash salad with kale and pomegranate, 81

C

Cabbage
cilantro lime slaw, 128
lightened-up pad thai in under 15 minutes, 125
updated Waldorf salad cups, 75

Caramel whiskey sauce, skillet apple crisp with, 215–16

Carrots, roasted, with honey butter, 92

Cashew and basil chicken lettuce wraps, 160

Cauliflower
with bacon, 99
sweet potato curry with, 61

Cheddar
baked gnocchi with three cheeses, 168
Cheddar biscuit-topped barbecue chicken pie, 187–88
spicy chipotle chicken enchiladas, 175–76
twice-baked breakfast potatoes, 40–41

Cheese. See also specific types
baked gnocchi with three cheeses, 168
loaded chorizo nachos, 189–91
petite lasagnas, 70–71

Cheesecakes, mini lemon-raspberry, with crumble topping, 217–19

Chia seeds: chocolate raspberry breakfast pudding, 25

Chicken
buffalo chicken egg rolls, baked, 72
cashew and basil chicken lettuce wraps, 160
Cheddar biscuit-topped barbecue chicken pie, 187–88
curry, with ginger and yogurt, 131–32
lemon roasted, with Moroccan couscous, 138–40

Chicken (cont.)
   and mushrooms, in mustard Marsala
      cream sauce, 141–42
   salad, Asian, 57
   Southwestern pulled chicken with
      cilantro lime slaw, 126–28
   souvlaki, with tzatziki and feta, 151–52
   spicy chipotle chicken enchiladas,
      175–76
   with sun-dried tomatoes and feta, 137
   tenders, Parmesan-crusted, with
      buttermilk ranch dressing, 149–50
   updated Waldorf salad cups, 75
Chickpeas
   spiced, chopped salad with tarragon-
      tahini dressing and, 48–49
   sweet potato curry with, 61
Chili, beef, ultimate, 66
Chipotle chicken enchiladas, spicy, 175–76
Chips, kale, 83
Chocolate
   chocolate hazelnut bread pudding with
      salted peanut butter sauce, 233–35
   chocolate raspberry breakfast pudding,
      25
   glaze, 228
   gooey chocolate chip cookie pie, 206–9
   peppermint cookies-and-cream fudge
      brownies, 230–32
Chorizo nachos, loaded, 189–91
Cilantro lime slaw, 128
Coconut
   coconut curry Brussels sprouts, 96
   coconut oatmeal cookies with caramel
      drizzle, 222–24
   lime coconut cream cups, 210–11
Cookies, coconut oatmeal, with caramel
      drizzle, 222–24
Couscous, Moroccan, lemon roasted
      chicken with, 138–40
Cream cheese
   glaze, maple-cinnamon, 17
   mini lemon-raspberry cheesecakes with
      crumble topping, 217–19
   vanilla cream cheese frosting, 205
Crisp, skillet apple, with whiskey caramel
      sauce, 215–16
Cuban pulled-pork sandwiches with
      caramelized onion and thyme mayo,
      181–82

Cucumber
   Greek salsa, 80
   tzatziki sauce, 152
Cupcakes, lemon poppy seed, with vanilla
      cream cheese frosting, 202–5
Curry
   chicken, with ginger and yogurt, 131–32
   coconut curry Brussels sprouts, 96
   sweet potato, 61

D
Desserts. See Sweets
Dinner, 106–63
   about, 129
   recipe list, 107–8
Doughnuts
   banana bread, baked, with maple-
      cinnamon cream cheese glaze, 16–17
   dulce de leche cream-filled, with
      chocolate glaze, 225–29
Dulce de leche cream-filled doughnuts
      with chocolate glaze, 225–29

E
Eggplant, white pizza with roasted garlic,
      ricotta, and, 179–80
Egg rolls, buffalo chicken, baked, 72
Egg(s)
   breakfast egg salad, 31
   creamy spinach, sun-dried tomato and
      artichoke omelet, 38
   frittata, all the greens, 33
   sweet potato hash, 43
   twice-baked breakfast potatoes, 40–41
Enchiladas, chipotle chicken, spicy,
      175–76
Entertaining. See Sharing

F
Farro, creamy, with white beans and kale,
      122
Feta
   chicken souvlaki with tzatziki and,
      151–52
   chicken with sun-dried tomatoes and,
      137
   Greek salsa, 80
   sweet potato hash, 43
Fish and seafood
   bagel and lox salad, 64–65

brown sugar and chili-rubbed salmon
      with avocado crema, 113–14
   halibut baked in parchment with
      pistachio mint pesto, 118–19
   jerk shrimp salad with mango and
      avocado, 109
   lemon-herb fish with crispy oven fries,
      110–11
Frittata, all the greens, 33
Frosting, vanilla cream cheese, 205

G
Garlic
   garlic bread, 134
   roasted, white pizza with ricotta,
      eggplant, and, 179–80
   smashed roasted garlic potatoes, 89
Ginger
   chicken curry with yogurt and, 131–32
   ginger apple compote, 159
Glaze
   chocolate, 228
   maple-cinnamon cream cheese, 17
Gnocchi, baked, with three cheeses, 168
Goat cheese
   all the greens frittata, 33
   arugula with orange segments, spiced
      walnuts and, 84
   turkey burgers with apple, caramelized
      onion and, 146–47
Gorgonzola. See also Blue cheese
   baked gnocchi with three cheeses,
      168
   shredded Brussels sprouts salad
      with bacon, apple and, 87
   updated Waldorf salad cups, 75
Granola parfaits, peanut butter, 34
Greek salsa, 80
Greek yogurt pancakes, 19
Green beans, sesame, 103
Greens. See also Kale; Spinach
   all the greens frittata, 33

H
Halibut baked in parchment with
      pistachio mint pesto, 118–19
Hash, sweet potato, 43
Hazelnut chocolate bread pudding with
      salted peanut butter sauce, 233–35

I

Italian salad, 50

J

Jerk shrimp salad with mango and
avocado, 109

K

Kale
butternut squash salad with
pomegranate and, 81
chips, 83
creamy farro with white beans and, 122
ribollita, 53

L

Lasagnas, petite, 70–71
Lemon
lemon cream risotto, 195
lemon-herb fish with crispy oven fries,
110–11
lemon poppy seed cupcakes with
vanilla cream cheese frosting, 202–5
lemon roasted chicken with Moroccan
couscous, 138–40
mini lemon-raspberry cheesecakes with
crumble topping, 217–19
Lettuce wraps, cashew and basil chicken,
160
Lime coconut cream cups, 210–11
Lox and bagel salad, 64–65
Lunch, 46–75
about, 62–63
recipe list, 47

M

Mango, jerk shrimp salad with avocado
and, 109
Maple-cinnamon cream cheese glaze,
17
Marshmallow whipped cream, peanut
butter mousse pie with, 200–201
Mayonnaise, thyme, 182
Meatballs and sauce, PJ's, 173–74
Meatloaf burgers with bacon, pepper Jack
and frizzled onions, 169–70
Mint: pistachio mint pesto, halibut baked
in parchment with, 118–19

Morning glory muffins, 37
Moroccan couscous, lemon roasted
chicken with, 138–40
Muffins, morning glory, 37
Mushrooms, chicken and, in mustard
Marsala cream sauce, 141–42

N

Nachos, chorizo, loaded, 189–91
Noodles. *See also* Pasta
pad thai, lightened-up, in under 15
minutes, 125

O

Oats
coconut oatmeal cookies with caramel
drizzle, 222–24
peanut butter granola parfaits, 34
tomorroats with blood orange mint
salsa, 26–27
Olives
beef puttanesca with garlic bread,
133–34
Greek salsa, 80
Omelet, creamy spinach, sun-dried
tomato and artichoke, 38
Onion(s)
caramelized, Cuban pulled-pork
sandwiches with thyme mayo and,
181–82
caramelized, turkey burgers with apple,
goat cheese and, 146–47
frizzled, 170
Orange(s)
arugula with spiced walnuts, goat
cheese and, 84
blood orange mint salsa, 27
mashed sweet potatoes with orange
zest and basil, 95
Orzo and tuna salad with Parmesan
and basil, 58

P

Pad thai, lightened-up, in under 15
minutes, 125
Pancakes, Greek yogurt, 19
Pancetta cream, spaghetti with Brussels
sprouts and, 145
Parfaits, peanut butter granola, 34

Parmesan
baked gnocchi with three cheeses, 168
and basil, tuna and orzo salad with, 58
Parmesan-crusted chicken tenders with
buttermilk ranch dressing, 149–50
Pasta
baked gnocchi with three cheeses, 168
petite lasagnas, 70–71
PJ's meatballs and sauce with, 173–74
spaghetti with Brussels sprouts and
pancetta cream, 145
tuna and orzo salad with Parmesan
and basil, 58
Peaches, grilled, spice-rubbed steak with
blue cheese and, 163
Peanut butter
dressing, Asian chicken salad with, 57
peanut butter granola parfaits, 34
peanut butter mousse pie with
marshmallow whipped cream,
200–201
salted peanut butter sauce, chocolate
hazelnut bread pudding with,
233–35
Pears: updated Waldorf salad cups, 75
Peas, sweet potato curry with, 61
Pecans, candied, 229
Peppermint cookies-and-cream fudge
brownies, 230–32
Pesto, pistachio mint, halibut baked in
parchment with, 118–19
Pie
barbecue chicken, Cheddar biscuit-
topped, 187–88
chocolate chip cookie, gooey, 206–9
peanut butter mousse, with
marshmallow whipped cream,
200–201
Pistachio mint pesto, halibut baked in
parchment with, 118–19
Pizza, white, with roasted garlic, ricotta
and eggplant, 179–80
Pomegranate, butternut squash salad
with kale and, 81
Pork
Cuban pulled-pork sandwiches with
caramelized onion and thyme mayo,
181–82
tenderloin, bacon-wrapped, with ginger
apple compote, 157–59

Potatoes
   crispy oven fries, lemon-herb fish with, 110–11
   smashed roasted garlic potatoes, 89
   twice-baked breakfast potatoes, 40–41
Pudding
   chocolate hazelnut bread pudding with salted peanut butter sauce, 233–35
   chocolate raspberry breakfast pudding, 25
   lime coconut cream cups, 210–11

R

Raspberries
   chocolate raspberry breakfast pudding, 25
   mini lemon-raspberry cheesecakes with crumble topping, 217–19
Ribollita, 53
Rice: lemon cream risotto, 195
Ricotta, white pizza with roasted garlic, eggplant, and, 179–80
Risotto, lemon cream, 195

S

Salad(s)
   about, 62–63
   arugula with orange segments, spiced walnuts and goat cheese, 84
   Asian chicken, 57
   bagel and lox, 64–65
   breakfast egg salad, 31
   butternut squash, with kale and pomegranate, 81
   chopped, with spiced chickpeas and tarragon-tahini dressing, 48–49
   cilantro lime slaw, 128
   Italian, 50
   jerk shrimp, with mango and avocado, 109
   shredded Brussels sprouts, with bacon, apple and Gorgonzola, 87
   tuna and orzo, with Parmesan and basil, 58
   Waldorf salad cups, updated, 75
Salmon
   bagel and lox salad, 64–65
   brown sugar and chili-rubbed, with avocado crema, 113–14
Salsa
   blood orange mint, 27

Greek, 80
Salted peanut butter sauce, chocolate hazelnut bread pudding with, 233–35
Sandwiches. See also Burgers
   Cuban pulled-pork, with caramelized onion and thyme mayo, 181–82
Sausage
   loaded chorizo nachos, 189–91
   turkey breakfast patties, 22
Seafood. See Fish and seafood
Sesame green beans, 103
Sharing, food for, 166–95
   about, 184–85
   recipe list, 167
Shrimp: jerk shrimp salad with mango and avocado, 109
Slaw, cilantro lime, 128
Soups and stews
   beef puttanesca with garlic bread, 134–35
   beef stew, 192–93
   ribollita, 53
   ultimate beef chili, 66
Southwestern pulled chicken with cilantro lime slaw, 126–28
Souvlaki, chicken, with tzatziki and feta, 151–52
Spaghetti with Brussels sprouts and pancetta cream, 145
Spinach
   all the greens frittata, 33
   creamy spinach, sun-dried tomato and artichoke omelet, 38
Squash: butternut salad with kale and pomegranate, 81
Steak, spice-rubbed, with grilled peaches and blue cheese, 163
Stew, beef, 192–93
Stir-fry, spicy tofu, with bok choy, 115–17
Sweet potatoes
   mashed, with orange zest and basil, 95
   sweet potato curry, 61
   sweet potato hash, 43
Sweets, 198–235
   about, 220–21
   recipe list, 199

T

Thyme mayonnaise, 182
Tofu stir-fry, spicy, with bok choy, 115–17
Tomato(es)
   beef puttanesca with garlic bread, 133–34
   creamy spinach, sun-dried tomato and artichoke omelet, 38
   Greek salsa, 80
   sun-dried, chicken with feta and, 137
Tomato sauce, PJ's meatballs and, 173–74
Tomorroats with blood orange mint salsa, 26–27
Tuna and orzo salad with Parmesan and basil, 58
Turkey
   burgers, with apple, caramelized onion and goat cheese, 146–47
   petite lasagnas, 70–71
   turkey breakfast patties, 22
Tzatziki sauce, 152

V

Vanilla cream cheese frosting, 205
Vegetables, 78–103. See also Salad(s); specific vegetables
   about, 90–91
   recipe list, 79

W

Waldorf salad cups, updated, 75
Walnuts, spiced, arugula with orange segments, goat cheese and, 84
Whiskey caramel sauce, skillet apple crisp with, 215–16

Y

Yogurt
   chicken curry with ginger and, 131–32
   chocolate raspberry breakfast pudding, 25
   Greek yogurt pancakes, 19
   peanut butter granola parfaits, 34
   tomorroats with blood orange mint salsa, 26–27
   tzatziki sauce, 152